metres	yards	metres	yards	metres	yards	metres	yards	metres	yards
85	93	170	186	460	503	80			
90	98½	180	197	465	508½	810	886	1400	1531
93	102	200	219	486	531½	851	930½	1430	1564
99	108	225	246	495	541½	860	940½	1440	1575
100	109½	230	251½	510	558	890	973½	1445	1580½
105	115	240	262½	540	590½	900	984½	1520	1662½
108	118	275	301	550	601½	945	1033½	1575	1722½
110	120½	295	322½	560	612½	1000	1093½	1580	1728
115	126	300	328	575	629	1035	1132	1600	1750
119	130	305	333½	600	656	1080	1181	1620	1771½
120	131	320	350	608	665	1100	1203	1715	1875½
130	142	340	372	610	667	1125	1230½	1765	1930
135	147½	360	394	660	722	1190	1301½	1800	1968½
139	152	375	410	689	753½	1200	1312½	1825	1996
140	153	400	437½	695	760	1215	1329	1975	2160
145	158½	405	443	700	765½	1225	1339½		
150	164	410	448½	729	797	1260	1378		
155	169½	440	481	745	815	1335	1460		
160	175	450	492	800	875	1340	1465½		

MW00612158

Knits For You *and* Your Dog

10 SWEATER DESIGNS TO MAKE FOR YOU AND YOUR PET

Anna-Karoliina Tetri
Annika Konttaniemi
Hanne Piirainen
Heli Rajavaara
Iris Tanttu
Marjukka Vuorisalo
Merja Ojanperä
Pirjo Iivonen
Tiia Reho
Védís Jónsdóttir

Quadrille, Penguin Random House UK, One Embassy Gardens, 8 Viaduct Gardens, London SW11 7BW

Quadrille Publishing Limited is part of the Penguin Random House group of companies whose addresses can be found at global.penguinrandomhouse.com

Penguin
Random House
UK

Copyright © Anna-Karoliina Tetri, Annika Konttaniemi, Hanne Piirainen, Heli Rajavaara, Iris Tanttu, Marjukka Vuorisalo, Merja Ojanperä, Pirjo Iivonen, Tiia Reho, Védís Jónsdóttir and Otava Publishing Company Ltd. 2025
Translation © Arthemaxx Translations 2025

Anna-Karoliina Tetri, Annika Konttaniemi, Hanne Piirainen, Heli Rajavaara, Iris Tanttu, Marjukka Vuorisalo, Merja Ojanperä, Pirjo Iivonen, Tiia Reho and Védís Jónsdóttir have asserted their right to be identified as the authors of this Work in accordance with the Copyright, Designs and Patents Act 1988.

Penguin Random House values and supports copyright. Copyright fuels creativity, encourages diverse voices, promotes freedom of expression and supports a vibrant culture. Thank you for purchasing an authorized edition of this book and for respecting intellectual property laws by not reproducing, scanning or distributing any part of it by any means without permission. You are supporting authors and enabling Penguin Random House to continue to publish books for everyone. No part of this book may be used or reproduced in any manner for the purpose of training artificial intelligence technologies or systems. In accordance with Article 4(3) of the DSM Directive 2019/790, Penguin Random House expressly reserves this work from the text and data mining exception.

First published in 2023 by Otava Publishing Company Ltd. with the Finnish title *Kaverille kans. Neuleita ja ihmisille*. Published in the English language by arrangement with Otava Publishing Company Ltd., Helsinki.

Published by Quadrille in 2025

www.penguin.co.uk

A CIP catalogue record for this book is available from the British Library.
ISBN 978 1 83783 271 2
10 9 8 7 6 5 4 3 2 1

Publishing Director Sarah Lavelle
Editorial Director Harriet Butt
Copy Editor Betsy Hosegood
Assistant Editor Oreolu Grillo
Technical Editor Heli Rajavaara
Designers Alicia House and Satu Kontinen
Photographer Anna Wallendahr
Illustrator Satu Kontinen (diagram on page 7 based on a template by Marjukka Vuorisalo)
Patterns and charts Anna-Karoliina Tetri, Annika Konttaniemi, Hanne Piirainen, Heli Rajavaara, Iris Tanttu, Marjukka Vuorisalo, Merja Ojanperä, Pirjo Iivonen, Tiia Reho, Védís Jónsdóttir
Production Director Stephen Lang
Senior Production Controller Martina Georgieva

Colour reproduction by F1

Printed in China by C&C Offset Printing Ltd

The authorised representative in the EEA is Penguin Random House Ireland, Morrison Chambers, 32 Nassau Street, Dublin D02 YH68.

Penguin Random House is committed to a sustainable future for our business, our readers and our planet. This book is made from Forest Stewardship Council® certified paper.

FSC
www.fsc.org
MIX
Paper | Supporting responsible forestry
FSC® C018179

Knits For You *and* Your Dog

10 SWEATER DESIGNS TO MAKE FOR YOU AND YOUR PET

Anna-Karoliina Tetri
Annika Konttaniemi
Hanne Piirainen
Heli Rajavaara
Iris Tanttu
Marjukka Vuorisalo
Merja Ojanperä
Pirjo Iivonen
Tiia Reho
Védís Jónsdóttir

Quadrille

Contents

Our best friends deserve knitwear made with love to keep them warm as the weather turns cold. The patterns in this book will help you to knit cosy sweaters for you and your human, canine and feline friends. Of course, knitting for you and your pet gives you the perfect opportunity to make matching outfits! But if coordinating knits isn't your thing, you'll find plenty of options. With unique patterns from ten renowned designers (nine from Finland and one from Iceland) ensuring a variety of styles, there's a jumper for everyone in this book. You'll definitely want to show these knits off!

Puru 11

Lykky 21

Luna 33

Aamusella 45

Risukko 57

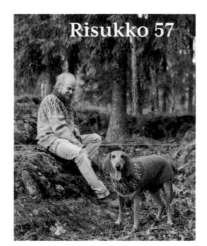

Semper in corde meo 69

Mitteli 87

Borg 107

Sydänystävä 97

Helix 117

Abbreviations

1/1 LC   1/1 left cross – slip 1 st onto a cable needle and hold at the front of the work, k1, k1 from the cable needle

1/1 RC   1/1 right cross – slip 1 st onto a cable needle and hold at the back of the work, k1, k1 from the cable needle

1/1 LPC   1/1 left purl cross – slip 1 st onto a cable needle and hold at the front of the work, p1, k1 from the cable needle

1/1 RPC   1/1 right purl cross – slip 1 st onto a cable needle and hold at the back of the work, k1, p1 from the cable needle

(For cables, the first number in the abbreviation indicates the number of stitches to be placed on the cable needle, the second indicates the number of stitches to knit from the main needle.)

C   colour

CC   contrast colour

cdd   centred double decrease: slip 2 sts onto the right-hand needle as if to knit them together, knit 1, then pass the slipped sts over the knitted st (2 sts decreased)

DS   double stitch

k   knit

k2tog   knit 2 sts together (1 st decreased)

k3tog   knit 3 sts together (2 sts decreased)

MC   main colour

M1k   make 1 st knitwise by picking up the strand between the stitches and knitting it (1 st increased)

M1p   make 1 purlwise by picking up the strand between the stitches and purling it (1 st increased)

M1L   left-leaning increase: pick up the strand between the two sts from the front, place it on the left-hand needle and then knit through the back loop

M1LP   purled left-leaning increase: as for M1L, but purl

M1R   right-leaning increase: pick up the strand between the two sts from behind, place it on the left-hand needle and then knit through the front loop

M1RP   purled right-leaning increase: as for M1R, but purl

p   purl

p2tog   purl 2 sts together (1 st decreased)

PM   place marker

RM   remove marker

RS   right side

SM   slip marker

ssk   slip, slip, knit decrease: slip 2 sts to the right-hand needle one by one knitwise, place them back on the left-hand needle then knit together through the back loop (1 st decreased)

sssk   slip, slip, slip, knit decrease: slip 3 sts to the right-hand needle one by one knitwise, place them back on the left-hand needle, then knit together through the back loop (2 sts decreased)

ssp   slip, slip, purl decrease: slip 2 sts to the right-hand needle one by one purlwise, place them back on the left-hand needle and purl together through the back loop (1 st decreased)

st(s)   stitch(es)

tbl   through the back loop

WS   wrong side

w&t   wrap and turn – slip the next st to the right-hand needle, bring yarn in front, return the stitch back to the left-hand needle

yo   yarn over – bring the yarn forward to increase 1 st

Measuring your dog

You will need the following measurements for the patterns in this book; some patterns require more measurements than others. Check the pattern to see the measurements you need, then measure your dog and add the ease specified in the pattern to the measurements. Before you begin, knit a swatch and adjust your needle size and/or yarn weight if necessary.

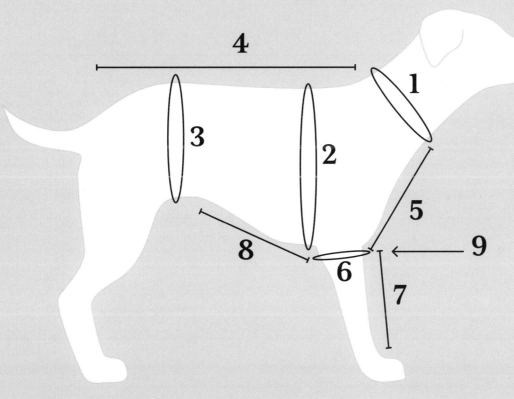

1. **Neck circumference:** measure approximately at the collar
2. **Chest circumference:** measure behind the front legs
3. **Waist circumference:** measure in front of the hind legs
4. **Back length:** measure from the collar to the base of the tail along the spine
5. **Front height:** measure the distance between the collar and front legs along the chest
6. **Front leg circumference:** measure at the elbow (where the leg meets the body)
7. **Sleeve length:** measure from the armpit to where you want the sleeve to end
8. **Front length to hem:** measure from the armpit to the hem, accounting for room for male dogs to urinate!
9. **Distance between front legs:** measure at the armpits

The Puru sweater was inspired by Popeye the Sailor and the brave Bull Terrier. The yarn was chosen with the dog in mind: this single-ply thick tweed yarn is forgiving on dog claws, although it does require a wool setting on the washing machine. The pattern has a characterful detail created with a third colour where the two main colours alternate – use this as an opportunity to use up leftover yarn or add a pop of brighter colour.

Puru

ᵛ ᵛ ᵛ ᵛ ᵛ

ANNIKA
KONTTANIEMI

IG annika_konttaniemi
RAVELRY AKonttaniemi

for humans

Shown in size S
Sizes: XS (S, M, L, XL) (2XL, 3XL, 4XL)
Recommended ease 10cm

∨∨∨∨∨∨∨∨∨∨∨∨∨∨∨∨∨∨∨∨∨∨∨∨∨∨∨∨∨∨∨∨∨∨

Measurements of finished sweater

Chest circumference: 88 (98.5, 109.5, 120)
(130.5, 141.5, 149.5, 160)cm

Waist circumference: 85.5 (96, 106.5, 117.5)
(128, 138.5, 146.5, 157.5)cm

Length from armpit to hem: 42 (43, 43, 44)
(45, 45, 47, 47)cm

Front length, neck to hem: 59 (61.5, 62.5, 66)
(69.5, 72.5, 76, 79)cm

Upper sleeve circumference: 34.5 (37.5, 38.5, 40)
(42.5, 44, 45.5, 48)cm

Wrist circumference: 26.5 (29.5, 29.5, 29.5)
(30.5, 30.5, 32, 33.5)cm

Underarm sleeve length: 42 (43, 43, 44)
(45, 45, 47, 47)cm

∨∨∨∨∨∨∨∨∨∨∨∨∨∨∨∨∨∨∨∨∨∨∨∨∨∨∨∨∨∨∨∨∨∨

Yarn

*Isager Aran Tweed (100% wool; 160m/100g) or equivalent
Aran-weight yarn*

C1 Navy 3 (3, 4, 4) (4, 5, 5, 5) hanks or 410 (460, 510,
560) (610, 660, 695, 745)m

C2: Grey 2 (2, 3, 3) (3, 3, 3, 4) hanks or 275 (305, 340,
375) (405, 440, 465, 495)m

C3: A little yarn that is the same weight as the main yarn,
approx. 50 (60, 65, 70) (75, 80, 85, 90) g or 80 (100, 105,
115) (120, 130, 140, 145)m

∨∨∨∨∨∨∨∨∨∨∨∨∨∨∨∨∨∨∨∨∨∨∨∨∨∨∨∨∨∨∨∨∨∨

Notions and tension (gauge)

Needles: 80–100cm circular needles in sizes 4mm (US 6)
and 5mm (US 8)

You will also need: Stitch markers, stitch holders or spare
yarn, tapestry needle

Tension: 15 sts and 22 rows = 10 x 10cm in stocking
(stockinette) stitch on 5mm (US 8) needles, lightly blocked.
Knit a swatch in colourwork and adjust your needle size
if necessary.

for dogs

Model: Bull Terrier
One size

∨∨∨∨∨∨∨∨∨∨∨∨∨∨∨∨∨∨∨∨∨∨∨∨∨∨∨∨

Neck circumference: 50.5cm

Chest circumference: 66.5cm

Waist circumference: 56cm

Back length: 50cm

Sleeve circumference: 20cm

Sleeve length from armpit: 10.5cm

Distance between front legs at armpits: 22.5cm

∨∨∨∨∨∨∨∨∨∨∨∨∨∨∨∨∨∨∨∨∨∨∨∨∨∨∨∨

*Isager Aran Tweed (100% wool; 160m/100g) or equivalent
Aran weight yarn*

C1: Navy 2 hanks or 320m

C2: Grey 1 hank or 160m

C3: A little yarn of equivalent weight to main yarn, approx.
40g or 65m

∨∨∨∨∨∨∨∨∨∨∨∨∨∨∨∨∨∨∨∨∨∨∨∨∨∨∨∨

Needles: 80–100cm circular needles in sizes 4mm (US 6)
and 5mm (US 8)

You will also need: Stitch markers, stitch holders or spare
yarn, tapestry needle

Tension: 15 sts and 22 rows = 10 x 10cm in stocking stitch
on 5mm (US 8) needles, lightly blocked. Knit a swatch in
colourwork and adjust your needle size if necessary.

Puru is a lovely, generous raglan sweater with a widened hem and sleeves, making it comfortable to wear over layers. It is knitted seamlessly from the bottom up and has minimal shaping, with only short rows in the neck and a slight A-line.

TIP

If you want to add texture to the knit, you can combine two or more lighter-weight yarns to make the C3 yarn.

Puru **for humans**

Body

Using 4mm (US 6) circular needles, cast on 138 (156, 172, 188) (204, 222, 234, 252) sts in C1. Join in the round and PM to mark the start of the round (centre back).

Work 10 rounds of *k1, p1* ribbing.

Swap to 5mm (US 8) circular needles. Purl 1 round, evenly decreasing 6 (8, 8, 8) (8, 10, 10, 12) sts. You should now have 132 (148, 164, 180) (196, 212, 224, 240) sts.

Continue the pattern in C3 from round 2 below.

Pattern:

Round 1: *Purl 1 round in C1.

Round 2: Knit 2 rounds in C3.

Knit 13 (14, 15, 16) (17, 18, 19, 20) rounds in C2.

Next round: Purl 1 round in C2.

Next round: Knit 1 round in C1.

In C1 and C3, knit the 2 rows of the chart. The chart repeats 33 (37, 41, 45) (49, 53, 56, 60) times per round.

Knit 13 (14, 15, 16) (17, 18, 19, 20) rounds in C1.*

Repeat *–*, until your work is 16cm long.

Next round: Continuing the pattern, knit 33 (37, 41, 45) (49, 53, 56, 60) sts, PM, knit 66 (74, 82, 90) (98, 106, 112, 120) sts, PM, knit to round marker.

Continue working the pattern while shaping the waist:

Decrease round 1: Knit to stitch marker, SM, knit 3 sts, k2tog, knit until 5 sts remain before the stitch marker, ssk, knit to stitch marker, SM, knit to the end of the round. *[2 sts decreased]*

Continue working the pattern for a further 11 rounds, then decrease again.

Decrease round 2: Knit until 5 sts remain before the stitch marker, ssk, knit to stitch marker, SM, knit to stitch marker, SM, knit 3 sts, k2tog, knit to the end of the round. *[2 sts decreased]*

You should now have 128 (144, 160, 176) (192, 208, 220, 236) sts.

Continue working the pattern until the body measures 42 (43, 43, 44) (45, 45, 47, 47)cm from the cast-on edge and the final knitted stripe is complete.

Separate the stitches for the armholes as follows:

*Knit to stitch marker, RM, knit 5 (5, 5, 6) (6, 6, 7, 7) sts, then transfer the last 10 (10, 10, 12) (12, 12, 14, 14) sts you just knitted onto a stitch holder *, repeat *–* once more, knit to the end of the round.

The front and back pieces now have 54 (62, 70, 76) (84, 92, 96, 104) sts. Set aside for now and knit the sleeves.

Sleeves

Using 4mm (US 6) circular needles, cast on 40 (44, 44, 44) (46, 46, 48, 50) sts in C1. Join in the round, PM to mark the start of the round.

Work 10 rounds of *k1, p1* ribbing.

Swap to 5mm (US 8) circular needles and begin following the pattern (see left). On the first round, increase 4 (4, 4, 4) (6, 6, 4, 6) sts at even intervals. You should now have 44 (48, 48, 48) (52, 52, 52, 56) sts.

Once the sleeve measures 25cm, begin increases while continuing to work the pattern.

Increase round: k1, M1k, knit until 1 st remains, M1k, knit the last st. *[2 sts increased]*

Repeat the increase round every 8 (8, 6, 6) (6, 6, 5, 5) rounds another 3 (3, 4, 5) (5, 6, 7, 7) times.

You should now have 52 (56, 58, 60) (64, 66, 68, 72) sts.

Continue working the pattern until the sleeve is 42 (43, 43, 44) (45, 45, 47, 47)cm long and you have knitted to the end of the last full stripe, as for the body.

Transfer the first 5 (5, 5, 6) (6, 6, 7, 7) sts and the last 5 (5, 5, 6) (6, 6, 7, 7) sts onto a stitch holder.

The sleeve now has 42 (46, 48, 48) (52, 54, 54, 58) sts.

Repeat for the other sleeve.

Yoke

Now join the body and the sleeves. If you wish, you can close the armpit sts using the three-needle cast-off (bind-off) during the round to join the sleeve and body armpit sts.

Note: The number of sts on the chart will not always line up perfectly at the raglan decreases.

Continuing in the pattern, and working from the beginning-of-round marker at the centre of the back, knit across the 27 (31, 35, 38) (42, 46, 48, 52) sts for the left back, PM, join the first sleeve by knitting the 42 (46, 48, 48) (52, 54, 54, 58) sts, PM, knit across the 54 (62, 70, 76) (84, 92, 96, 104) sts for the front, PM, join the second sleeve by knitting the 42 (46, 48, 48) (52, 54, 54, 58) sts, PM, knit to the end of the round.

You should now have 192 (216, 236, 248) (272, 292, 300, 324) sts.

Continue working the pattern for 5 (4, 2, 2) (1, 0, 0, 0)cm and then begin the raglan decreases:

Round 1 (decrease): *Knit the pattern until 2 sts remain before the stitch marker, k2tog, SM, k1, ssk, knit until 3 sts remain before the stitch marker, k2tog, k1, SM, ssk*, repeat *–* once, knit to the end of the round. *[8 sts decreased]*

Round 2: Knit the pattern until the end of the round.

Repeat rounds 1 and 2 another 12 (15, 17, 17) (19, 19, 19, 20) times.

Sizes – (–, M, L) (XL, 2XL, 3XL, 4XL):

Next round (decrease): *Follow the pattern until 2 sts remain before the stitch marker, k2tog, SM, knit to stitch marker, SM, ssk*, repeat *–* once, knit to the end of the round. *[4 sts decreased]*

Next round: Knit the pattern until the end of the round.

Repeat the last 2 rounds 0 (0, 0, 3) (5, 9, 11, 13) times.

You should now have 88 (88, 88, 88) (88, 92, 92, 100) sts. Now knit the short rows to raise the back neck.

Neck raise

(and final raglan decreases)

All short rows are knitted in the same colour as was used in the previous row.

Row 1 (RS): Knit until 2 sts remain before the stitch marker, k2tog, SM, k1, ssk, knit until 3 sts remain before the stitch marker, k2tog, k1, SM, ssk, k8, turn.

Row 2 (WS): DS, purl to round marker, SM, purl until 2 sts remain before the stitch marker, ssp, SM, p1, p2tog, purl until 3 sts remain before the stitch marker, ssp, p1, SM, p2tog, p8, turn.

Row 3 (RS): DS, knit to round marker, SM, knit until 2 sts remain before the stitch marker, k2tog, SM, k1, ssk, knit until 3 sts remain before the stitch marker, k2tog, k1, SM, ssk, k3, turn.

Row 4 (WS): DS, purl to round marker, SM, purl until 2 sts remain before the stitch marker, ssp, SM, p1, p2tog, purl until 3 sts remain before the stitch marker, ssp, p1, SM, p2tog, p3, turn.

Row 5 (RS): DS, knit to round marker, SM.

You should now have 72 (72, 72, 72) (72, 76, 76, 84) sts.

Neck

In the next round, evenly decrease 4 (4, 2, 2) (2, 4, 4, 4) sts. Purl 1 round.

Cut C2 and C3 and continue to the end in C1. Swap to 4mm (US 6) circular needles and work 16 rounds of *k1, p1* ribbing.

Cast off using a very stretchy casting off method. Fold the ribbing over double to the wrong side. Sew very loosely, as sewn sts are much less flexible than knitted sts, and you need to retain some flexibility in the neckline so that it can stretch across your head as you put on the sweater.

Finishing

Sew in the ends. Steam block the sweater, or wet it and leave it to dry flat.

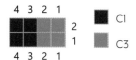

Puru **for dogs**

Pattern:

Round 1: Purl in C1.

Rounds 2–3: Knit in C3.

Rounds 4–17: Knit in C2.

Round 18: Purl in C2.

Round 19: Knit in C1.

Rounds 20–21: Knit the chart in C1 and C3.

Rounds 22–35: Knit in C1.

Body

Using 4mm (US 6) needles cast on 76 sts in C1. Join in the round, PM to mark the start of the round (centre front). Work 10 rounds of *k1, p1* ribbing.

Swap to 5mm (US 8) circular needles. Purl 1 round, evenly increasing 12 sts. You should now have 88 sts.

Begin working the pattern (see above), starting at round 2. Knit 3 rounds of the pattern and then use short rows to raise the height of the chest as explained below, first placing a stitch marker at the centre of the round (centre back).

Short rows (knitted in the same colour as the previous row):

Row 1 (RS): Knit until 4 sts remain before the marker, turn.

Row 2 (WS): DS, purl to round marker, SM, purl until 4 sts remain before the marker, turn.

Row 3 (RS): DS, knit to round marker, SM, knit until 4 sts remain before the DS, turn.

Row 4 (WS): DS, purl to the round marker, SM, purl until 4 sts remain before the DS, turn.

Repeat rows 3 and 4 twice more.

Row 9 (RS): DS, knit to round marker, SM.

Knit one round in which you work every DS as a single st.

Next round: Continue to work the pattern, evenly increasing 12 sts. You should now have 100 sts.

Continue to work the pattern and knit another set of short rows as before when you are on round 23 of the pattern. You can remove the stitch marker at the centre back of the round when you have completed the short row shaping. Begin raglan increases for the sleeve holes.

Sleeve holes for the front legs

Set-up for raglan increases:

Continue to work the pattern and knit 10 sts, PM, knit 3 sts, PM, knit 74 sts, PM, knit 3 sts, PM, knit until the end of the round (4 new stitch markers placed to mark the raglan seams for the front legs).

Round 1 (increase): *Follow the pattern to the stitch marker, M1R, SM, k1, M1L, knit until 1 st remains before stitch marker, M1R, k1, SM, M1L*, repeat *–* once, knit to the end of the round. [8 sts increased]

Round 2: Knit the pattern until the end of the round.

Repeat rounds 1–2 another 6 times. You should now have 156 sts (122 sts in the body and 17 sts on each sleeve). Continue to knit the pattern, only increasing on the sleeves:

Next round (increase): *Knit to the stitch marker, SM, k1, M1L, knit until 1 st remains before the stitch marker, M1R, k1, SM*, repeat *–* once, knit to the end of the round.

Next round: Knit the pattern to the end of the round.

Repeat the last 2 rounds 3 more times. You should have 172 sts (122 sts in the body and 25 sts on each sleeve).

Separate the sleeves from the body:

Continue to knit the pattern.

Next round: Knit to stitch marker, SM, transfer the next 25 sts onto a stitch holder, cast on 5 armpit sts, SM, knit to the stitch marker, SM, transfer the next 25 sts onto a stitch holder, cast on 5 armpit sts, SM, knit to the end of the round.

The sweater for dogs is knitted seamlessly in the round from the neck. Stitches for the sleeves are made using raglan increases. Short rows are used to shape the chest and lower back.

Note: Remember which round of the pattern you are on, as the sleeves will need to continue the pattern from the same round when you come to knit them later on.

The body now has 132 sts. The stitch markers remain in the same place to mark where the waist decreases will be positioned.

Waist decreases

Decrease round: *Follow the pattern until 2 sts remain before the stitch marker, k2tog, SM, knit 5 sts, SM, ssk*, repeat *–* once, knit to the end of the round. *[4 sts decreased]*

Repeat the decreases every round for another 11 rounds. You should now have 84 sts.

You can now remove the other stitch markers, but leave the round marker where it is. Continue to knit the pattern until the sweater measures 23cm from the armpit.

Lower-back shaping

The back is lengthened using short rows. These look neatest when placed in the solid colour parts of the pattern.

Short rows:

Row 1 (RS): Knit until 2 sts remain before the marker, turn.

Row 2 (WS): DS, purl until 2 sts remain before the marker, turn.

Row 3 (RS): DS, knit until 4 sts remain before the DS in the previous row, turn.

Row 4 (WS): DS, purl until 4 sts remain before the DS in the previous row, turn.

Repeat rows 1–2 twice more.

Continue for another 3 rows following the pattern. Remember to work DSs as 1 st.

Cut C2 and C3 and continue to the end in C1.

Purl 1 round.

Swap to 4mm (US 6) circular needles and work in *k1, p1* ribbing. One more set of short rows will be added to the ribbing as follows.

Short rows:

Row 1 (RS): Knit until 2 sts remain before the round marker, turn.

Row 2 (WS): DS, knit until 2 sts remain before the round marker, turn.

Row 3 (RS): DS, knit until 4 sts remain before the DS in the previous row, turn.

Row 4 (WS): DS, knit until 4 sts remain before the DS in the previous row, turn.

Repeat rows 3–4 once more.

Continue in ribbing, working DSs as single sts. Loosely cast (bind) off.

Sleeves

Begin to knit the sleeve from the centre of the armpit sts.

Using 5mm (US 8) needles and the relevant colour in the pattern, pick up and knit 2 sts, knit 25 sleeve sts, then pick up and knit another 3 sts. Join in the round, PM. You should now have 30 sts.

Knit another 6cm following the pattern.

Swap to 4mm (US 6) needles and work 10 rounds of *k1, p1* ribbing or until the sleeve is the desired length.

Loosely cast off.

Repeat for the other sleeve.

Finishing

Sew in the ends. Steam block the sweater, or wet it and leave it to dry flat.

	4	3	2	1	
2					
1					
	4	3	2	1	

■ C1
■ C3

TIP

∨ ∨ ∨ ∨ ∨

Puru is especially suitable
for dogs with large chests
and narrow waists, and its
measurements can be adjusted
to better suit your dog by
changing the number of short
rows or by making the back and
sleeves longer.

Lykky

In the northern Ostrobothnian dialect of Finland, 'lykky' means both a stitch and good luck. Knitters are a lucky bunch who can use the same word to describe both the craft itself and the joy it brings.

∨∨∨∨∨

HANNE
PIIRAINEN
FB & IG
@puikoillapeltolassa

for humans

Sizes: XS (S, M, L) (XL, 2XL, 3XL, 4XL)

Recommended ease 5cm

~~~~~~~~~~~~~~~~~~~~~~~~~~~~~~~~~~~~~

Measurements of finished sweater

Chest circumference: 73.5 (82, 90, 101)
(109, 117.5, 128, 136.5)cm

Length from armpit to hem: 44 (45, 46, 47)
(47, 48, 48, 49)cm

Front length, neck to hem: 59.5 (62.5, 65, 68.5)
(70, 73.5, 75, 77.5)cm

Upper sleeve circumference: 27 (28.5, 30.5, 31.5)
(34, 37.5, 41.5, 44)cm

Wrist circumference: 18 (18, 18, 18) (22, 22, 25.5, 25.5)cm

Underarm sleeve length: 49 (50, 51, 52)
(52, 52, 52, 52)cm

~~~~~~~~~~~~~~~~~~~~~~~~~~~~~~~~~~~~~

Yarn

*Markus Company 8 ply (75% wool, 25% polyamide;
200m/100g) or equivalent DK weight yarn*

MC: Rain Drum 4 (4, 5, 5) (5, 5, 6, 6) skeins or 800 (800,
900, 900) (1000, 1000, 1200, 1200)m

CC1: Fuchsia Purple 1 (1, 1, 1) (1, 1, 1, 1) skein or 200 (200,
200, 200) (200, 200, 200, 200)m

CC2: Autumn Glory 1 (1, 1, 1) (1, 1, 1, 1) skein or 200 (200,
200, 200) (200, 200, 200, 200)m

~~~~~~~~~~~~~~~~~~~~~~~~~~~~~~~~~~~~~

Notions and tension (gauge)

Needles: 80–100cm and 40cm circular needles in sizes
3.5mm (US 4) and 4.5mm (US 7), and double-pointed
needles in size 3.5mm (US 4)

You will also need: Stitch markers, stitch holders or spare
yarn, cable needle, tapestry needle

Tension: 22 sts and 26 rows = 10 x 10cm in stocking
(stockinette) stitch on 4.5mm (US 7) needles, lightly
blocked. Knit a swatch in colourwork and adjust your needle
size if necessary.

for dogs

Model: Labrador Retriever

One size

Recommended ease 0–2cm

Neck circumference: 48cm

Chest circumference: 95.5cm

Back length: 73.5cm

Front height: 29cm

*Markus Company 8 ply (75% wool, 25% polyamide;
200m/100g) or equivalent DK weight yarn*

MC: Army Green 4 skeins or 800m

CC1: Golden Glow 1 skein or 200m

CC2: Autumn Glory 1 skein or 200m

Needles: 40–60cm circular needles in sizes 3.5mm
(US 4) and 4.5mm (US 7), and double-pointed needles in
sizes 3.5mm (US 4) and 4.5mm (US 7)

You will also need: Stitch markers, stitch holders or spare
yarn, cable needle, tapestry needle

Tension: 22 sts and 26 rows = 10 x 10cm in stocking stitch
on 4.5mm (US 7) needles, 25 sts and 30 rows = 10 x 10cm
in ribbing on 3.5mm (US 4) needles, lightly blocked. Knit
a swatch in colourwork and adjust your needle size if
necessary.

Knitted from hem to neck, the human version of this seamless sweater has raglan sleeves and combines both colourwork and cable knitting.

Lykky for humans

Body

Using 3.5mm (US 4) circular needles, cast on 160 (180, 200, 220) (240, 260, 280, 300) sts in the MC. Join in the round, PM to mark the start of the round (right side seam).

Work *k2, p2* ribbing for 15 rounds.

Swap to 4.5mm (US 7) needles and knit 1 round in stocking stitch. Then begin the colourwork from row 1 of chart A; repeat the 10-stitch pattern 16 (18, 20, 22) (24, 26, 28, 30) times per round. Once you have knitted all 81 rows of the chart, cut the CCs.

Sizes S, XL and 4XL only:
Knit 1 round in the MC.

Sizes XS, L and 3XL only:
Knit 1 round using the MC, evenly increasing 2 sts.

Sizes M and 2XL only:
Knit 1 round using the MC, evenly decreasing 2 sts.

You should now have 162 (180, 198, 222) (240, 258, 282, 300) sts.

Begin to work the textured knitting in chart C. Work the chart until the sweater measures 44 (45, 46, 47) (47, 48, 48, 49)cm.

Next round: Cast (bind) off 2 (2, 3, 3) (3, 4, 4, 5) sts, k77 (86, 93, 105) (114, 121, 133, 140) sts following chart C (sweater back), cast off 4 (4, 6, 6) (6, 8, 8, 10) sts, k77 (86, 93, 105) (114, 121, 133, 140) sts following chart C (sweater front), cast off 2 (2, 3, 3) (3, 4, 4, 5) sts.

Make a note of which row of chart C you are on. You will continue from the following round when you knit the yoke. Set aside the sts for the body and begin the sleeves.

Sleeves

Using 3.5mm (US 4) double-pointed needles (or long circular needles if you're using the magic-loop technique), cast on 40 (40, 40, 40) (48, 48, 56, 56) sts in the MC. Join in the round, PM to mark the start of the round. Work *k2, p2* ribbing for 15 rounds.

Swap to 4.5mm (US 7) needles and knit 1 round in stocking stitch, evenly increasing 0 (0, 0, 0) (2, 2, 4, 4) sts in the round. You should now have 40 (40, 40, 40) (50, 50, 60, 60) sts.

Begin the colourwork with row 1 of chart B and repeat the pattern 4 (4, 4, 4) (5, 5, 6, 6) times per round.

Knit all 20 rows of the chart. Cut the CCs and continue to the end of the sleeve using the MC.

Knit 1 round in stocking stitch then begin the increases.

Increase round 1: K1, M1R, knit until 1 st remains, M1L, k1. *[2 sts increased]*

Repeat the increase row another 8 (10, 12, 13) (11, 15, 14, 17) times every 4th round.

Knit 4 rounds in stocking stitch and then knit the final increase.

Increase round 2: K1, M1R, knit to the end of the round. *[1 st increased]*

You now have 59 (63, 67, 69) (75, 83, 91, 97) sts.

Continue knitting in stocking stitch until the sleeve measures 49 (50, 51, 52) (52, 52, 52, 52)cm.

Next round: Cast off 2 (2, 3, 3) (3, 4, 4, 5) sts, knit 55 (59, 61, 63) (69, 75, 83, 87) sts, cast off 2 (2, 3, 3) (3, 4, 4, 5) sts.

Repeat for the other sleeve.

Yoke

Now join the body and the sleeves.

Place the sts for the body back onto 4.5mm (US 7) needles and continue using the MC.

Knit the 77 (86, 93, 105) (114, 121, 133, 140) sts for the back, following chart C and continuing from where you left off, PM, knit the 55 (59, 61, 63) (69, 75, 83, 87) sts for the sleeve, PM, knit the 77 (86, 93, 105) (114, 121, 133, 140) sts for the front following chart C, PM, knit the 55 (59, 61, 63) (69, 75, 83, 87) sts for the sleeve, PM. The start of the round is at the right back raglan seam.

You should now have 264 (290, 308, 336) (366, 392, 432, 454) sts.

Round 1 (decrease): *k1, k2tog, knit chart C until 3 sts remain before the marker, ssk, k1, SM, k1, k2tog, knit until 3 sts remain before the marker, ssk, k1, SM*, repeat *–* once more. *[8 sts decreased]*

Round 2: *Knit chart C to marker, SM, knit to marker, SM*, repeat *–* once more.

Repeat rounds 1–2 another 19 (22, 22, 24) (25, 26, 28, 29) times.

You now have 104 (106, 124, 136) (158, 176, 200, 214) sts.

Now knit the decreases on the front and back only:

Next round (decrease): *k1, k2tog, knit chart C until 3 sts remain before the marker, ssk, k1, SM*, knit to marker, SM*, repeat *–* once more. *[4 sts decreased]*

Repeat the previous round another 0 (0, 4, 6) (8, 12, 12, 14) times.

You should now have 100 (102, 104, 108) (122, 124, 148, 154) sts.

Sizes XS, M, L, 2XL and 3XL only:
Knit 1 round.

Sizes S, XL and 4XL only:
Knit 1 round, evenly decreasing 2 sts.
You now have 100 (100, 104, 108) (120, 124, 148, 152) sts.

Next knit the short rows for the neck.

Short rows:

Note: All short rows are worked in *k2, p2* ribbing.

Row 1 (RS): Work ribbing to marker, RM, continue to marker, SM, work 4 sts, turn.

Row 2 (WS): DS, work to marker, SM, continue to round marker, SM, continue to marker, SM, work 4 sts, turn.

Row 3 (RS): DS, work ribbing to marker, SM, continue to round marker, SM, continue to marker, SM, turn.

Row 4 (WS): DS, work to round marker, SM, work to marker, RM, turn.

Row 5 (RS): DS, work ribbing to round marker, SM.

Swap to 3.5mm (US 4) needles.

Next row (RS) Work ribbing until the end of the round, always working DSs as single sts.

Continue *k2, p2* ribbing for 15 rounds.

Cast off using a stretchy cast-off method.

Finishing

Weave in all of the ends and sew the armpit holes closed.

Lightly steam block the sweater.

Chart A, body

Chart B, sleeve

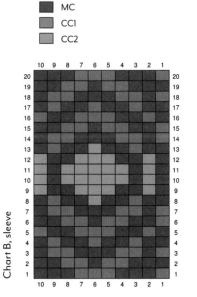

Chart C, body and yoke

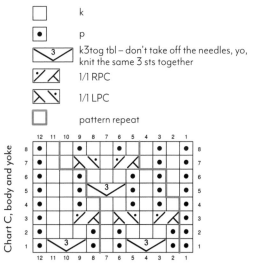

Legend:
- ■ MC
- ■ CC1
- ■ CC2

- ☐ k
- • p
- ⟋3⟍ k3tog tbl – don't take off the needles, yo, knit the same 3 sts together
- 1/1 RPC
- 1/1 LPC
- ☐ pattern repeat

Lykky for dogs

Neck

Using 4.5mm (US 7) circular needles, cast on 120 sts in the MC. Join in the round, PM to mark the start of the round (front right).

Rounds 1–40: k1, *p2, k2*, repeat *–* until 3 sts remain, p2, k1.

Body

On the next round, increase 16 sts as follows: work 28 sts in ribbing, PM (front left), *k5, M1R* twice, *k6, M1R* 12 times, *k5, M1R* twice.

You should now have 136 sts (28 sts on the belly and 108 sts on the back).

Round 1 (increase): M1R, work ribbing to the marker, M1L, SM, knit to the end of the round following chart A (the pattern repeats 17 times). *[2 sts increased]*

Round 2: Work ribbing to the marker (ribbing continues in the increases), SM, knit to the end of the round following chart A.

Repeat rounds 1–2 another 19 times.

You should now have 176 sts (68 sts on the belly and 108 sts on the back).

Sleeve gussets

Knit the sleeve gussets as follows:

Round 1 (increase): M1R, work 19 sts of ribbing, M1R, PM, p2, PM, M1L, work 26 sts of ribbing, M1R, PM, p2, PM, M1L, work 19 sts of ribbing, M1L, SM, knit to the end of the round following chart A. *[6 sts increased]*

Round 2: *Work ribbing to marker, SM, p2, SM* twice, work ribbing to marker, SM, knit to the end of the round following chart A.

Round 3 (increase): M1R, *work ribbing to marker, M1R, SM, p2, SM, M1L* twice, work ribbing to marker, M1L, SM, knit to the end of the round following chart A.
[6 sts increased]

Round 4: *Work ribbing to marker, SM, p2, SM* twice, work ribbing to marker, SM, knit to the end of the round following chart A.

Repeat rounds 3 and 4 another 5 times. You should now have 218 sts (110 sts on the belly and 108 sts on the back).

Separate the sleeve stitches:

Next round: *Work ribbing to marker, SM, p2, SM, work 7 sts of ribbing. Move the last 16 sts you worked onto a stitch holder, remove the two markers in that set of 16 sts.* M1, work 26 sts of ribbing, M1. Repeat *–*. Work ribbing to marker, SM, knit to the end of the round following chart A. SM, work ribbing until the sleeve hole. Move the sts for the back (160 sts) onto a stitch holder; do not cut the yarn.

In MC, work the 28 sts between the sleeve holes flat, knitting 10cm of ribbing. Place the sts onto a stitch holder. Continue to work the sts for the back in rows.

Row 1 (WS): M1, work ribbing to marker, SM, knit chart A to marker, SM, work ribbing to the end of the row, M1, turn. *[2 sts increased]*

Row 2 (RS): Work ribbing to marker, SM, work chart A to marker, SM, work ribbing to the end of the row, turn.

Chart A

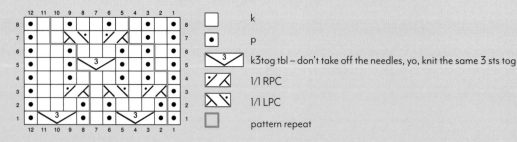

☐	k
•	p
◩3	k3tog tbl – don't take off the needles, yo, knit the same 3 sts tog
▨	1/1 RPC
◪	1/1 LPC
☐	pattern repeat

The sweater for dogs is worked from the neck down, with ribbing for a comfortable fit.

Row 3 (WS): Work ribbing to marker, SM, work chart A to marker, SM, work ribbing to the end of the row, turn.
Work for 8cm, repeating rows 2 and 3, ending on a RS row: Work ribbing to marker, RM, work chart A to marker, RM, work ribbing to the end of the row, PM (this is the new round marker). Do not turn the work.
Now join the sts for the belly and back.
Next round (RS): Cast on 8 sts at the sleeve, work the sts for the belly in ribbing, cast on 8 sts at the second sleeve, PM, knit to the end of the round.
You should now have 206 sts (44 sts in the belly, 162 sts in the back).
Next round (decrease/increase): k2tog, knit to marker, SM, k27, *M1R, k27* 5 times.
You should now have 210 sts (43 sts in the belly, 167 sts in the back).
Begin charts B and C on pages 28–29.
Next round: Knit chart B to the marker, repeating the 10-stitch pattern between the red guidelines 4 times, SM, knit chart C to the marker, repeating the 10-stitch pattern between the red guidelines 11 times.
Repeat the round until you have knitted all rows of the chart, decreasing as directed in chart C.
You should now have 162 sts (43 sts in the belly, 119 sts in the back).
Swap to 3.5mm (US 4) needles.
Next round (decrease): Knit to marker, SM, k2tog, knit until 2 sts remain, ssk. *[2 sts decreased]*
Work 1 round of *k2, p2* ribbing.
Next round: RM, work ribbing to marker, RM, work 58 sts of ribbing, PM (this is the new round marker at the centre of the back).

Now knit the short rows for the back.
Short rows:
Row 1 (RS): Work 10 sts of ribbing, turn.
Row 2 (WS): DS, work ribbing to marker, SM, work 10 sts of ribbing, turn.
Row 3 (RS): DS, work ribbing to marker, SM, work ribbing to DS, work the DS as a single st, work 10 sts of ribbing, turn.
Row 4 (WS): DS, work ribbing to marker, SM, work ribbing to DS, work the DS as a single st, work 10 sts of ribbing, turn.
Repeat rows 3 and 4 another 5 times.
Next row (RS): DS, work ribbing to marker, SM.
Work another 5 rounds of *k2, p2* ribbing (work the DS as a single st on the first row).
Cast (bind) off using a stretchy cast-off method.

Sleeves

Using 3.5mm (US 4) needles and the MC, beginning from the centre back of the sleeve hole, pick up and knit 4 sts from the back edge and 13 sts from the outer edge. Knit the 16 sts that you previously set aside, pick up and knit 15 sts from the inner edge of the sleeve hole and the remaining 4 sts from the back edge (52 sts in total). Join in the round and PM to mark the start of the round (the back of the leg).
Work *k2, p2* ribbing for 10cm.
Cast off using a stretchy cast-off method.
Repeat for the other sleeve.

Finishing

Sew in the ends.
Lightly steam block the sweater.

Chart B, belly

Chart C, back (Note that the chart is in two parts)

28

MC
CC1
CC2
k2tog
ssk
no stitch
pattern repeat

Both the human and
dog version of the Lykky
sweater are designed to
be practical.

TIP

∨ ∨ ∨ ∨ ∨

The ribbing on the dog version of Lykky helps
to achieve a good fit, making this design ideal
for dogs of many sizes and breeds.

Luna

A summer day is dawning, there are beads of dew on the grass, and the cool night air lingers. A morning walk with your dog is a peaceful moment together, giving you time to wake up and get ready for the day's adventures.

HELI
RAJAVAARA

IG helirajavaara
RAVELRY
Heli Rajavaara

Luna I is a relaxed-fit raglan sweater with three-quarter length sleeves that is knitted from the top down. The version shown to the left has a charming colourwork pattern around the hem.

Like Luna I above, Luna II is knitted from the top down. It has the same relaxed fit and three-quarter length sleeves, but in this version the pretty colourwork is on the yoke.

I

Shown in size S

Sizes: XS (S, M, L) (XL, 2XL, 3XL, 4XL)

Recommended ease 10cm

∨∨∨∨∨∨∨∨∨∨∨∨∨∨∨∨∨∨∨∨∨∨∨

Measurements of finished sweater

Chest circumference: 87.5 (94.5, 105.5, 112.5,) (123.5, 134.5, 145.5, 156.5)cm

Length from armpit to hem: 31.5 (31.5, 32.5, 32.5) (33.5, 33.5, 34.5, 34.5)cm

Front length, neck to hem: 53.5 (54.5, 57.5, 58.5) (60.5, 62, 64.5, 65.5)cm

Upper sleeve circumfrence: 28 (28, 31, 32) (36.5, 39, 42, 45.5)cm

Wrist circumference: 23.5 (23.5, 27.5, 27.5) (31, 32.5, 36.5, 38)cm

Underarm sleeve length: 30 (30, 31, 31) (32, 32, 33, 33)cm

∨∨∨∨∨∨∨∨∨∨∨∨∨∨∨∨∨∨∨∨∨∨∨

Yarn

Aara Aatos (75% superwash merino, 25% nylon; 225m/100g) or equivalent DK weight yarn

MC: Luja 4 (5, 5, 5) (6, 6, 7, 7) hanks or 860 (945, 1035, 1125) (1215, 1340, 1340, 1520)m

CC1: Koru 1 (1, 1, 1) (1, 1, 1, 1) hank or 45 (50, 55, 55) (60, 65, 70, 75)m

CC2: Helmi (1, 1, 1) (1, 1, 1, 1) hank or 35 (40, 45, 45) (50, 55, 60, 65)m

∨∨∨∨∨∨∨∨∨∨∨∨∨∨∨∨∨∨∨∨∨∨∨

Notions and tension (gauge)

Needles: 80–100cm circular needles in sizes 3mm (US 2.5) and 3.5mm (US 4)

You will also need: Stitch markers, stitch holders or spare yarn, tapestry needle

Tension: 22 sts and 30 rows = 10 x 10cm in stocking (stockinette) stitch on 3.5mm (US 4) needles, lightly blocked. Knit a swatch in colourwork and adjust your needle size if necessary.

II

Shown in size S

Sizes: XS (S, M, L) (XL, 2XL, 3XL, 4XL)

Recommended ease 15–20cm

∨∨∨∨∨∨∨∨∨∨∨∨∨∨∨∨∨∨∨∨∨∨∨

Chest circumference: 91 (98, 111, 120) (129, 138, 149, 158)cm

Length from armpit to hem: 33 (33, 34, 34) (35, 35, 36, 36)cm

Front length, neck to hem: 53 (54, 56, 58) (60, 62, 64, 65)cm

Circumference of upper sleeve: 31 (32.5, 34.5, 38) (41, 42.5, 44.5, 46.5)cm

Wrist circumference: 24.5 (27.5, 30, 32.5) (35.5, 35.5, 38, 38)cm

Underarm sleeve length: 30cm (all sizes)

∨∨∨∨∨∨∨∨∨∨∨∨∨∨∨∨∨∨∨∨∨∨∨

Aara Aatos (75% superwash merino, 25% nylon; 225m/100g) or equivalent DK weight yarn

MC: Luja 4 (4, 5, 6) (7, 7, 8, 9) hanks or 810 (900, 1035, 1190) (1370, 1575, 1765, 1975)m

CC1: Koru 1 (1, 1, 1) (1, 1, 1, 1) hank or 70 (75, 85, 90) (100, 110, 120, 135)m

CC2: Helmi (1, 1, 1) (1, 1, 1, 1) hank or 35 (40, 45, 45) (50, 55, 60, 70)m

∨∨∨∨∨∨∨∨∨∨∨∨∨∨∨∨∨∨∨∨∨∨∨

Needles: 80–100cm circular needles in sizes 3mm (US 2.5) and 3.5mm (US 4)

You will also need: Stitch markers, stitch holders or spare yarn, tapestry needle

Tension: 22 sts and 30 rows = 10 x 10cm in stocking stitch on 3.5mm (US 4) needles, lightly blocked. Knit a swatch in colourwork and adjust your needle size if necessary.

Luna I

Yoke

Using 3mm (US 2.5) circular needles, cast on 92 (96, 104, 112) (112, 120, 128, 140) sts in the MC. Join in the round, PM to mark the start of the round (centre back). Work *k2, p2* ribbing for 3cm.

Swap to 3.5mm (US 4) circular needles and knit 1 round, then place stitch markers at the raglan seams as follows: K12 (14, 16, 18) (18, 20, 22, 24), PM, k22 (20, 20, 20) (20, 20, 20, 22), PM, k24 (28, 32, 36) (36, 40, 44, 48), PM, k22 (20, 20, 20) (20, 20, 20, 22), PM, knit to the end of the round.

Next raise the back neck using short rows and begin the raglan increases.

Short rows:

Row 1 (RS): *Knit until 1 st remains before the marker, M1R, k1, SM, k1, M1L* twice, k2, turn.

Row 2 (WS): DS, *purl to marker, SM* twice, purl to round marker, SM, *purl until 1 st remains before the marker, M1RP, p1, SM, p1, M1LP* twice, p2, turn.

Row 3 (RS): DS, *knit to marker, SM* twice, knit to round marker, SM, *knit until 1 st remains before the marker, M1R, k1, SM, k1, M1L* twice, knit to DS and knit it as a single st, k2, turn.

Row 4 (WS): DS, *purl to marker, SM* twice, purl to round marker, SM, *purl until 1 st remains before the marker, M1RP, p1, SM, p1, M1LP* twice, purl to DS and purl it as a single st, p2, turn.

Repeat rows 3–4 another 1 (1, 1, 1) (2, 2, 2, 2) time(s).

Next row (RS): DS, *knit to marker, SM* twice, knit to round marker. Do not turn the work.

You should now have 116 (120, 128, 136) (144, 152, 160, 172) sts.

Continue working in stocking (stockinette) stitch in the round and knit the raglan increases (knit the DSs as single sts in the first round).

Round 1 (increase): *Knit until 1 st remains before the marker, M1R, k1, SM, k1, M1L* 4 times, knit until the end of the round. [8 sts increased]

Round 2: *Knit to marker, SM* 4 times, knit to the end of the round.

Round 3 (increase): *Knit until 1 st remains before the marker, M1R, k1, SM, knit to marker, SM, k1, M1L* twice, knit until the end of the round. [4 sts increased]

Round 4: As for round 2.

Repeat rounds 1–4 another 15 (16, 17, 18) (19, 20, 21, 22) times.

You should now have 308 (324, 344, 364) (384, 404, 424, 448) sts, 94 (102, 110, 118) (124, 132, 140, 148) sts on the front and back, and 60 (60, 62, 64) (68, 70, 72, 76) sts on each sleeve.

Sizes 2XL (3XL, 4XL) only:

Repeat rounds 1–2 twice more.

You should now have 420 (440, 464) sts: 136 (144, 152) sts on the front and back, and 74 (76, 80) sts on each sleeve.

All sizes:

Continue in stocking stitch until the work measures 22 (23, 25, 26) (27, 28.5, 30, 31)cm from the front neck.

Body

Separate the sleeves and body:

Next round: RM, knit to marker, RM, place 60 (60, 62, 64) (68, 74, 76, 80) sleeve sts onto a stitch holder, RM, cast on 1 (1, 3, 3) (6, 6, 8, 10) sts, PM (this is the new round marker), cast on 1 (1, 3, 3) (6, 6, 8, 10) sts, knit the front sts to marker, RM, place the next 60 (60, 62, 64) (68, 74, 76, 80) sleeve sts onto a stitch holder, RM, cast on 2 (2, 6, 6) (12, 12, 16, 20) sts, knit to round marker. You should now have 192 (208, 232, 248) (272, 296, 320, 344) sts.

Continue working in stocking stitch in the MC until the work measures 17 (17, 18, 18) (19, 19, 20, 20)cm from the armpit.

Knit the colourwork pattern following the chart. The pattern repeats 24 (26, 29, 31) (34, 37, 40, 43) times per round. Knit all 35 rows of the chart and then cut the CCs.

Knit 4 rounds in stocking stitch in the MC.

Swap to 3mm (US 2.5) needles. Work *k2, p2* ribbing for 3cm.

Cast (bind) off using a stretchy cast-off method.

Sleeves

Move the 60 (60, 62, 64) (68, 74, 76, 80) sleeve sts that are reserved on a stitch holder onto 3.5mm (US 4) circular needles. Starting from the middle of the armpit and working in the MC, pick up and knit 1 (1, 3, 3) (6, 6, 8, 10) sts, knit the sleeve sts, pick up and knit 1 (1, 3, 3) (6, 6, 8, 10) sts, PM. Join in the round. You should now have 62 (62, 68, 70) (80, 86, 92, 100) sts.

Knit 5 rounds in stocking stitch and then begin the decreases.

Decrease round: k1, k2tog, knit until 3 sts remain, ssk, k1. *[2 sts decreased]*

Repeat the decrease round another 4 (4, 3, 4) (5, 6, 5, 7) times every 14th (14th, 14th, 14th) (10th, 8th, 10th, 8th) round. You should now have 52 (52, 60, 60) (68, 72, 80, 84) sts.

Continue in stocking stitch until the length of the sleeve from the armpit is 27 (27, 28, 28) (29, 29, 30, 30)cm. If you would like longer sleeves, continue in stocking stitch until the sleeve is 3cm shorter than the desired length.

Swap to 3mm (US 2.5) needles and work *k2, p2* ribbing for 3cm.

Cast off using a stretchy cast-off method.

Repeat for the other sleeve.

Finishing

Sew in the ends.

Wet the sweater and carefully squeeze out the excess water without stretching it. You can do this by placing it inside a towel.

Adjust the sweater until it matches the finished measurements and then leave to dry flat.

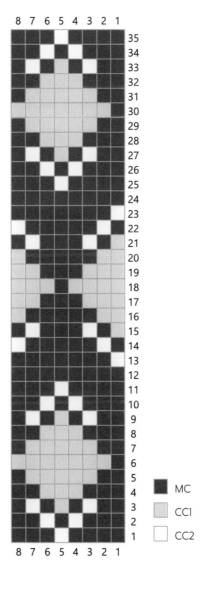

Luna II

Yoke

Using 3mm (US 2.5) needles, cast on 90 (96, 102, 108) (114, 120, 126, 132) sts in the MC. Join in the round, PM to mark the start of the round (centre back).

Work *k3, p3* ribbing for 3cm. Swap to 3.5mm (US 4) needles and knit 1 round.

Next round (increase): *k2, M1L, k1, M1L* until the end of the round. You should now have 150 (160, 170, 180) (190, 200, 210, 220) sts.

Next raise the back neck using short rows.

Short rows:

Row 1 (RS): k36 (38, 40, 44) (48, 50, 52, 54), turn.

Row 2 (WS): DS, purl to round marker, SM, p36 (38, 40, 44) (48, 50, 52, 54), turn.

Row 3: DS, knit to DS and knit it as a single st, k2, turn.

Row 4: DS, purl to DS and purl it as a single st, p2, turn.

Repeat rows 3–4 another 2 (2, 2, 2) (2, 3, 3, 3) times.

Next row (RS): DS, knit to round marker. Do not turn the work.

Knit 2 rounds (work the DS as a single st), and then knit an increase round.

Next round (increase): *k2, M1L* until the end of the round. You should now have 225 (240, 255, 270) (285, 300, 315, 330) sts.

Knit 1 (1, 2, 4) (6, 8, 8, 8) round(s) in stocking (stockinette) stitch and then knit the following increase round:

Size XS: k1, *k3, M1L, k2, M1L, k2, M1L*, repeat *–*, until 7 sts remain, k3, M1L, k2, M1L, k2. [95 sts increased, 320 sts total]

Size S: Repeat *k3, M1L, k2, M1L* until the end of the round. [96 sts increased, 336 sts total]

Size M: Repeat *k3, M1L* 12 times, *k3, M1L, k2, M1L* 36 times, *k3, M1L* 13 times. [97 sts increased, 352 sts total]

Size L: **K5, M1L, repeat *k2, M1L, k3, M1L* 26 times**, repeat **–** one more time. [106 sts increased, 376 sts total]

Size XL: k1, M1L, k2, M1L, k2, M1L, repeat *k2, M1L, k3, M1L* until the end of the round. [115 sts increased, 400 sts total]

Size 2XL: **k5, M1L, repeat *k2, M1L, k3, M1L* 14 times**, repeat **–** three more times. [116 sts increased, 416 sts total]

Size 3XL: k5, M1L, repeat *k2, M1L, k3, M1L* until the end of the round. [125 sts increased, 440 sts total]

Size 4XL: **k1, M1L, k2, M1L, k2, M1L, repeat *k2, M1L, k3, M1L* 32 times**, repeat **–** one more time. [134 sts increased, 464 sts total]

Knit 1 round and then begin the colourwork following the chart. The pattern repeats 40 (42, 44, 47) (50, 52, 55, 58) times per round. Knit all 35 rows of the chart and then cut the CCs.

Knit 1 round in the MC and then knit the final increase round for sizes M upwards:

Size M: k32, M1L, repeat *k16, M1L* 9 times, k32, M1L, repeat *k16, M1L* 9 times. [20 sts increased, 372 sts total]

Size L: Repeat *k15, M1L, k16, M1L, k16, M1L* 8 times. [24 sts increased, 400 sts total]

Size XL: k32, M1L, repeat *k16, M1L* 23 times. [24 sts increased, 424 sts total]

Size 2XL: k11, M1L, repeat *k15, M1L* until the end of the round. [28 sts increased, 444 sts total]

Size 3XL: k4, M1L, repeat *k16, M1L* 27 times, k4. [28 sts increased, 468 sts total]

Size 4XL: Repeat *k20, M1L, k19, M1L, k19, M1L* 8 times. [24 sts increased, 488 sts total]

Continue stocking stitch in the MC until the yoke measures 20 (21, 22, 24) (25, 27, 28, 29)cm from the front neck.

Body

Separate the sleeves and body:

In the MC, k48 (51, 58, 62) (66, 70, 75, 79) sts, place the next 64 (66, 70, 76) (80, 82, 84, 86) sleeve sts onto a stitch holder, cast on 2 (3, 3, 4) (5, 6, 7, 8) sts, PM (this is the new round marker), cast on 2 (3, 3, 4) (5, 6, 7, 8) sts, knit the 96 (102, 116, 124) (132, 140, 150, 158) sts for the front, place the next 64 (66, 70, 76) (80, 82, 84, 86) sleeve sts onto a stitch holder, cast on 4 (6, 6, 8) (10, 12, 14, 16) sts, knit to marker (the old round marker), RM, knit to round marker. You should now have 200 (216, 244, 264) (284, 304, 328, 348) sts.

Continue in stocking stitch in the MC until the work measures 30 (30, 31, 31) (31, 32, 33, 33)cm from the armpit.

Next round:

Sizes M (2XL, 3XL): Knit *k122 (152, 164), M1R* twice. *[2 sts increased]*

Sizes XS (XL): Knit *k98 (140), k2tog* twice. *[2 sts decreased]*

All sizes:

Swap to 3mm (US 2.5) needles. Work *k3, p3* ribbing for 3cm.

Cast (bind) off using a stretchy cast-off method.

Sleeves

Move the 64 (66, 70, 76) (80, 82, 84, 86) sleeve sts onto 3.5mm (US 4) circular needles. Starting from the middle of the armpit and working in the MC, pick up and knit 2 (3, 3, 4) (5, 6, 7, 8) sts, knit the sleeve sts, pick up and knit 2 (3, 3, 4) (5, 6, 7, 8) sts, PM. Join in the round. You should now have 68 (72, 76, 84) (90, 94, 98, 102) sts.

Knit 5 rounds in stocking stitch and then begin the decreases.

Decrease round: K1, k2tog, knit until 3 sts remain, ssk, k1. *[2 sts decreased]*

Repeat the decrease round another 6 (5, 4, 5) (5, 7, 6, 8) times every 10th (10th, 12th, 10th) (10th, 8th, 10th, 8th) round. You should now have 54 (60, 66, 72) (78, 78, 84, 84) sts.

Continue in stocking stitch until the length of the sleeve from the armpit is 27cm.

Swap to 3mm (US 2.5) needles and work *k3, p3* ribbing for 3cm.

Cast off using a stretchy cast-off method.
Repeat for the other sleeve.

Finishing

Sew in the ends.

Wet the sweater and gently squeeze out the excess water without stretching it. You can do this by placing it inside a towel.

Adjust the sweater until it matches the finished measurements and leave to dry flat.

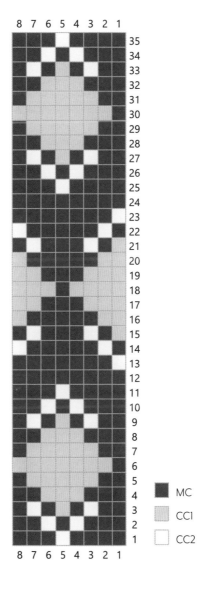

for dogs

Model: Jack Russell Terrier (size 1)
Sizes: 1 (2, 3)

~~~~~~~~~~~~~~~~~~~~~~~~~~~~~~~

Measurements of finished sweater
Neck circumference: 30 (32.5, 43.5)cm
Chest circumference: 40 (49, 72.5)cm
Waist circumference: 35.5 (43.5, 68)cm
Back length: Adjustable

~~~~~~~~~~~~~~~~~~~~~~~~~~~~~~~

Yarn
Aara Aatos (75% superwash merino, 25% nylon; 225m/100g)
or equivalent DK weight yarn
MC: Luja 2 (2, 2) hanks or 240 (295, 450)m
CC1: Koru 1 (1, 1) hank or 12 (15, 22)m
CC2: Helmi 1 (1, 1) hank or 5 (7, 10)m

~~~~~~~~~~~~~~~~~~~~~~~~~~~~~~~

Notions and tension (gauge)
Needles: 80–100cm (32–40in) circular needles (if you
use the magic loop technique) in sizes 3mm (US 2.5) and
3.5mm (US 4), double-pointed needles in size 3.5mm (US
4) for the sleeves (if you don't use the magic loop technique)
You will also need: Stitch markers, spare yarn,
tapestry needle
Tension: 22 sts and 30 rows = 10 × 10cm in stocking
(stockinette) stitch on 3.5mm (US 4) needles, lightly
blocked. Knit a swatch in colourwork and adjust your needle
size if necessary.

Neck
Using 3mm (US 2.5) circular needles, cast on 66 (72,
96) sts in the MC. Join in the round, PM to mark the start
of the round (centre belly).
Work *k3, p3* ribbing for 3cm.

Body
Swap to 3.5mm (US 4) circular needles. Continue in the
MC and knit 2 rounds in stocking stitch. Then begin
the increases.
Increase round 1: Repeat *k6, M1R* until the end of the
round. *[11 (12, 16) sts increased]*
Knit 3 rounds in stocking stitch.
Increase round 2: Repeat *k7, M1R* until the end of the
round. *[11 (12, 16) sts increased]*
Knit 5 rounds in stocking stitch.
Sizes 2 and 3 only:
Increase round 3: Repeat *k8, M1R* until the end of the
round. *[0 (12, 16) sts increased]*
Knit 5 rounds in stocking stitch.
Size 3 only:
Increase round 4: Repeat *k9, M1R* until the end of the
round. *[0 (0, 16) sts increased]*
Knit 5 rounds in stocking stitch.
You should now have 88 (108, 160) sts.
All sizes:
Now shape the chest using short rows:
Row 1 (RS): k18 (22, 32), turn.
Row 2 (WS): DS, purl to round marker, SM, p18 (22,
32), turn.
Row 3: DS, knit to round marker, SM, knit until 4 sts
remain before the previous DS, turn.
Round 4: DS, purl to round marker, SM, purl until 4 sts
remain before the previous DS, turn.
Repeat rows 3–4 another 2 (3, 4) times.
Next row (RS): DS, knit to round marker, SM.
Then knit 1 round, knitting all of the DSs as single sts.
Continue in stocking stitch until the work reaches the
front legs. Then make the holes for the sleeves.

Next round: k9 (11, 14), knit the next 9 (11, 16) sts onto spare yarn, move them back onto the left-hand needle and then knit them again with the working yarn, knit until 18 (22, 30) sts remain, knit the next 9 (11, 16) sts onto spare yarn, move them back onto the left-hand needle and then knit them again with the working yarn, knit to the end of the round.

Knit 1 round in stocking stitch stitch and then begin the decreases.

Decrease round: K1, k2tog, knit until 3 sts remain, ssk, k1. *[2 sts decreased]*

Continue in stocking stitch and repeat the decrease round another 1 (2, 2) time(s) every 5cm. You should now have 84 (102, 154) sts.

Continue in stocking stitch until the work is 8cm shorter than the desired finished length. On the last round, evenly decrease 4 (6, 2) sts.

You should now have 80 (96, 152) sts.

Knit the colourwork pattern following the chart. The pattern repeats 10 (12, 19) times per round. Knit all 11 rows of the chart and then cut the CCs and continue in the MC.

Knit 4 rounds in stocking stitch. On the last round, evenly decrease 2 (0, 2) sts. You should now have 78 (96, 150) sts.

Swap to 3mm (US 2.5) circular needles and work *k3, p3* ribbing for 3cm.

Cast (bind) off using a stretchy cast-off method.

Sleeves

Knit the sleeves in the MC. Carefully remove the spare yarn and use 3.5mm (US 4) circular needles to pick up 9 (11, 16) sts from the top and the bottom. Also pick up 2 sts from both edges. Join in the round, PM to mark the start of the round. You should now have 22 (26, 36) sts.

Sizes 1 and 2 only:

Next round: Knit *k9 (11), k2tog* twice. *[2 sts decreased]*

Size 3 only:

Next round: Knit to the end of the round.

All sizes:

Work *k2, p2* ribbing until the sleeves are the desired length.

Cast off using a stretchy cast-off method.

Repeat for the other sleeve.

Finishing

Sew in the ends.

Wet the sweater and gently squeeze out the excess water without stretching it. You can do this by placing it inside a towel.

Adjust the sweater until it matches the finished measurements and leave to dry flat.

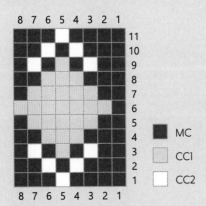

TIP

∨ ∨ ∨ ∨ ∨

The sweater for your favourite walking
companion can be adjusted to suit
your pet's measurements to ensure a
comfortable fit, even for large dogs.
You may wish to shorten the sweater
for male dogs.

Some of my favourite memories are of frequent walks with my four-legged friend in the yard of my childhood home at the dawn of a new day. I loved to hear the birds sing the morning chorus, and to see the blooming red clovers, as well as the sparkly beads of dew adorning the cobwebs and bushes. I endeavoured to capture that fresh feeling in the Aamusella sweater.

The base colour for this sweater is grey in honour of my beloved Keeshonds, which have been cherished family members throughout my childhood and into adulthood. The details of the sweater incorporate elements from those unforgettable summer mornings spent with my now dearly departed canine friends.

Aamusella

IRIS
TANTTU
samoilevatsukkaset.com
IG & FB
samoilevatsukkaset

for humans

Shown in size M–L
Sizes: XS–S (M–L, XL–2XL, 3XL–4XL)
Recommended ease 0–2cm

∨∨∨∨∨∨∨∨∨∨∨∨∨∨∨∨∨∨∨∨∨∨∨∨∨∨∨∨

Measurements of finished sweater

Chest circumference: 76 (95, 114.5, 133.5)cm
Length from armpit to hem: 40.5 (40.5, 43.5, 43.5)cm
Front length, neck to hem: 61 (62, 66, 67.5)cm
Upper sleeve circumference: 28.5 (36, 43, 48.5)cm
Wrist circumference: 24 (24, 28.5, 28.5)cm
Underarm sleeve length: 46.5 (48.5, 50.5, 51.5)cm

∨∨∨∨∨∨∨∨∨∨∨∨∨∨∨∨∨∨∨∨∨∨∨∨∨∨∨∨

Yarn

*Drops Karisma (100% superwash wool; 100m/50g) or
equivalent DK/Aran weight yarn*
MC1: 44 Light grey 5 (6, 7, 9) skeins or 460
(575, 689, 804)m
MC2: 21 Medium grey 5 (7, 8, 9) skeins or 486
(608, 729, 851)m
CC1: 19 White 1 (1, 2, 2) skein(s) or 80 (99, 119, 139)m
CC2: 68 Light sky blue 1 (1, 1, 1) skein or 36 (44, 53, 62)m
CC3: 30 Light denim blue 1 (1, 1, 1) skein or 41 (51, 61, 71)m
CC4: 33 Medium pink 1 (1, 1, 1) skein or 27 (33, 40, 47)m
CC5: 71 Silver pink 1 (1, 1, 1) skein or 27 (33, 40, 47)m
CC6: 47 Forest green 1 (1, 1, 2) skein(s) or 62
(77, 93, 108)m

*Lankava Lysti (75% superwash wool, 25% polyamide;
200m/100g) or equivalent DK/Aran weight yarn*
CC7: 862 Pistachio 1 (1, 1, 1) skein or 57 (71, 85, 99)m

∨∨∨∨∨∨∨∨∨∨∨∨∨∨∨∨∨∨∨∨∨∨∨∨∨∨∨∨

Notions and tension (gauge)

Needles: 80–100cm circular needles and either double-pointed needles or 40cm circular needles in sizes 3.5mm (US 4) and 4mm (US 6)
You will also need: Stitch markers, stitch holders or spare yarn, tapestry needle
Tension: 21 sts and 28 rows = 10 x 10cm in stocking (stockinette) stitch on 4mm (US 6) needles, lightly blocked. Knit a swatch in colourwork and adjust your needle size if necessary.

for dogs

Model: Border Terrier
One size

Neck circumference: 38cm
Chest circumference: 52.5cm
Waist circumference: 46.5cm
Back length: 40cm (adjustable)
Sleeve length: 17.5cm (adjustable)

Yarn

*Drops Karisma (100% superwash wool; 100m/50g) or
equivalent DK/Aran weight yarn*
MC1: 44 Light grey 1 skein or 90m
MC2: 21 Medium grey 2 skeins or 160m
CC1: 19 White 1 skein or 30m
CC2: 68 Light sky blue 1 skein or 20m
CC3: 30 Light denim blue 1 skein or 20m
CC4: 33 Medium pink 1 skein or 20m
CC5: 71 Silver pink 1 skein or 20m
CC6: 47 Forest green 1 skein or 20m
*Lankava Lysti (75% superwash wool, 25% polyamide;
200m/100g) or equivalent DK/Aran weight yarn*
CC7: 862 Pistachio 1 skein or 30m

Needles: 40cm circular needles and double-pointed needles in sizes 3.5mm (US 4) and 4mm (US 6)
You will also need: Stitch markers (one openable), stitch holders or spare yarn, tapestry needle
Tension: 21 sts and 28 rows = 10 x 10cm in stocking stitch on 4mm (US 6) needles, lightly blocked. Knit a swatch in colourwork and adjust your needle size if necessary.

This sweater is knitted in the round from the top down. The colourwork on the yoke is peppered with bobbles to depict beads of dew on cobwebs.

Aamusella for humans

Yoke

Using 3.5mm (US 4) double-pointed needles or the shorter circular needles cast on 96 (120, 144, 168) sts in MC1. Join in the round, PM to mark the start of the round (centre back). Begin to knit chart A, working the pattern repeats 8 (10, 12, 14) times per round. If you like, you can place stitch markers to mark each pattern repeat. Knit all 20 rows of the chart.

Swap to the shorter 4mm (US 6) circular needles. Now knit chart B; the pattern repeats 8 (10, 12, 14) times per round. Knit increases according to the chart. Once you have knitted all 53 rows of the chart, cut the CCs and continue in MC1 (if you have marked repeats with stitch markers, you can remove them now, but leave the round marker where it is).

Note for rounds 40–53 of chart B: You can Swiss darn or duplicate the sts marked 'S', and crochet the bobbles onto the work once it's finished.

You should now have 208 (260, 312, 364) sts. Swap to the longer 4mm (US 6) circular needles.

Knit 1 round in stocking (stockinette) stitch, evenly increasing 8 (10, 12, 14) sts.

Knit 3 (5, 9, 13) rounds in stocking stitch.

Knit 1 round in stocking stitch, evenly increasing 8 (10, 12, 14) sts.

You should now have 224 (280, 336, 392) sts.

Continue in stocking stitch until the work measures 21 (24, 26, 27)cm from the bottom edge of the ribbing.

Body

Separate the body and sleeves:

RM, k33 (41, 50, 59), place 46 (58, 68, 78) sts onto a stitch holder or spare yarn (right sleeve), cast on 6 (8, 10, 11) sts, PM (this is the new round marker), cast on 6 (8, 10, 11) sts, k66 (82, 100, 108), place 46 (58, 68, 78) sts onto a stitch holder or spare yarn (left sleeve), cast on 12 (16, 20, 22) sts, knit to the end of the round. You should now have 156 (196, 240, 280) sts.

Knit 1 round, evenly increasing 4 (4, 0, 0) sts. You should now have 160 (200, 240, 280) sts.

Knit 5 rounds in stocking stitch and then begin chart C. The pattern repeats 32 (40, 48, 56) times per round. Once you have knitted all 38 rows of the chart, cut MC1 and continue in MC2 until the work measures 20 (20, 23, 23)cm from the armpit.

Now knit chart D (see page 50); the pattern repeats 8 (10, 12, 14) times per round. CC4 and CC5, and part of CC6 and CC7 are Swiss-darned onto the work afterwards (sts marked with 'S'). Knit all 43 rows of chart D. Cut the CCs and continue in MC2. Knit 2 rounds in stocking stitch.

Swap to the longer 3.5mm (US 4) circular needles and work 5cm of *k1, p1* ribbing. Cast (bind) off using a stretchy cast-off method.

Sleeves

Place the 46 (58, 68, 78) reserved sleeve sts onto 4mm (US 6) double-pointed needles or the shorter circular needles. Starting from the centre of the armpit, pick up and knit 6 (8, 10, 11) sts in MC1, pick up and knit 1 st from

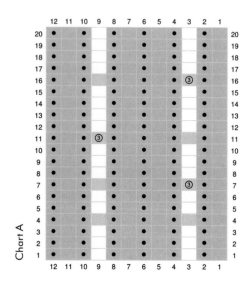

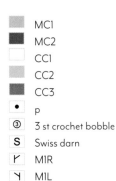

- MC1
- MC2
- CC1
- CC2
- CC3
- • p
- ③ 3 st crochet bobble
- S Swiss darn
- ⌐ M1R
- ⌐ M1L
- no stitch

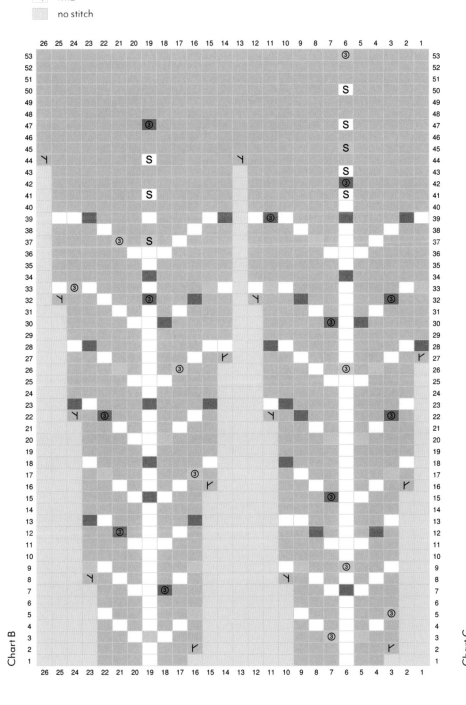

Chart B

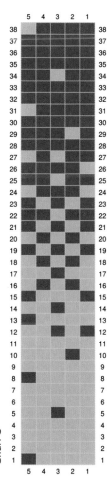

Chart C

between the armpit and sleeve sts. Knit the sleeve sts, pick up and knit 1 st from between the sleeve and armpit sts, pick up and knit 6 (8, 10, 11) sts from the armpit, PM. You should now have 60 (76, 90, 102) sts.

Knit 1cm in stocking (stockinette) stitch.

For sizes M–L: Evenly increase 4 sts on the final round.

For sizes 3XL–4XL: Evenly decrease 2 sts on the final round.

You should now have 60 (80, 90, 100) sts.

Knit charts C1, C and C2 as follows:

Next round: Chart C1 once, chart C 8 (12, 14, 16) times, chart C2 once.

Repeat this round until you have knitted all 38 rows of the charts.

Cut MC1 and continue in MC2. At the same time, continue decreases at both edges every – (4th, 5th, 3rd)

round another – (9, 9, 14) times. (No decrease for the smallest size.) You should now have 48 (50, 60, 60) sts.

Continue in stocking stitch until the sleeve measures 28 (30, 32, 33)cm from the armpit.

Size XS–S: Evenly increase 2 sts on the final round. Now knit chart E; the chart repeats 5 (5, 6, 6) times per round. CC4 and CC5 are Swiss-darned onto the work afterwards (sts marked 'S'). Knit all 29 rows of the chart and then cut the CCs and continue in MC2.

Knit 1 round in stocking stitch and then swap to 3.5mm (US 4) double-pointed needles or the short circular needles. Work *k1, p1* ribbing for 8cm. Cast (bind) off using a stretchy cast-off method. Repeat for the other sleeve.

Finishing

Weave the ends into the wrong side of the work and gently wet the sweater in lukewarm water. Carefully squeeze out the excess water and shape the sweater to its final measurements. Dry flat.

Chart D

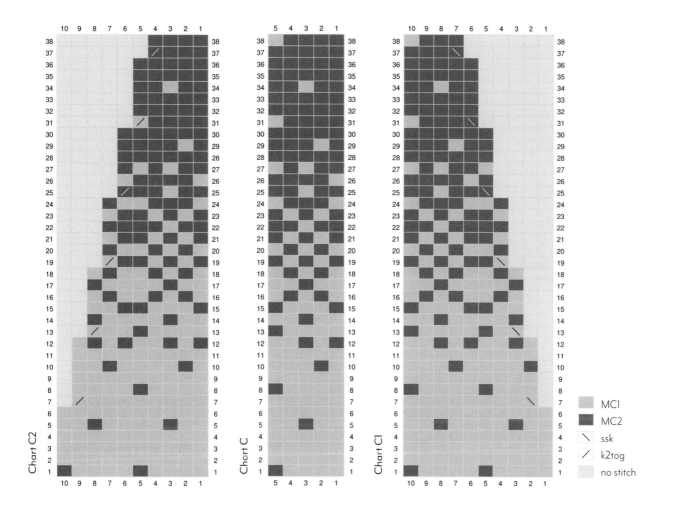

Chart C2

Chart C

Chart C1

MC1
MC2
ssk
k2tog
no stitch

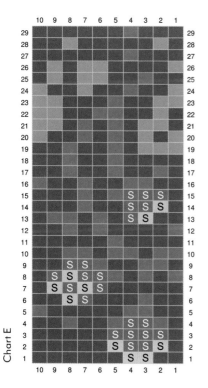

Chart E

MC2
CC5
CC4
CC6
CC7
S Swiss darn

Aamusella **for dogs**

Body

Using 3.5mm (US 4) double-pointed needles, cast on 80 sts in MC1 and divide them evenly across the four needles: 20 sts per needle. Join in the round, PM to mark the start of the round.

Begin to knit chart A; the pattern repeats 5 times per round. After round 10, swap to 4mm (US 6) double-pointed or circular needles and continue to knit the chart. Knit the increases where marked on the chart. Work all 34 rows of the chart.

Note: If you like, you can Swiss darn the sts marked 'S' in rows 25–34 of the chart afterwards.

You should now have 110 sts.

Immediately follow with chart B; the pattern repeats 11 times per round. Knit all 17 rows of the chart and then cut MC1 and continue in MC2.

Holes for the sleeves:

k7, place 20 sts onto a stitch holder, cast on 16 sts, k56, place 20 sts onto a stitch holder, cast on 16 sts, knit to the end of the round. This is the gap between the front legs and the start of a new round.

You should now have 102 sts.

Now knit 5 rounds in stocking (stockinette) stitch in MC2. Then begin the decreases.

Next round (decrease): k2tog, knit until 2 sts remain, k2tog. [2 sts decreased]

Knit 4 rounds in stocking stitch and repeat the decrease round one more time. You should now have 98 sts.

Continue in stocking stitch until the work measures 8cm from the sleeve hole.

Now knit chart C (see pages 54–55). Note the chart covers both male and female dog versions; the adjustments for the male dog are shown in red.

Male dog:

Knit 5 rounds of chart C in the round and then begin working flat in rows. Cast (bind) off to form the edges following the red lines on the chart.

TIP

⌄ ⌄ ⌄ ⌄ ⌄

This pattern is designed for a small dog, and can be adapted for your own pooch by adjusting the length of the body and the upper part of the sleeves, which has no colourwork.

For male dogs, the sweater is shorter under the belly, while for female dogs, it is knitted in the round to the end.

Note: Swap the round marker for a stitch marker that you can open and close. Knit all 32 rows of the chart.

You should now have 38 sts. Cut the CCs and continue in MC2.

Pick up 68 sts from the edges to knit the edge ribbing. You should now have 106 sts.

Knit to the stitch marker in the centre belly and then knit another row.

Swap to 3.5mm (US 4) circular needles and work *k1, p1* ribbing for 2cm. Cast (bind) off using a stretchy cast-off method.

Female dog:

Knit in the round following chart C and ignoring the instructions in red. Knit all 32 rows of the chart and then cut the CCs and continue in MC2.

Knit 1 round.

Swap to 3.5mm (US 4) circular needles and work *k1, p1* ribbing for 2cm. Cast off using a stretchy cast-off method.

Sleeves

Place the 20 reserved sts onto 4mm (US 6) double-pointed needles. In MC2 and starting from the centre of the cast-on sts, pick up and knit 8 sts, pick up and knit another st from in between this st and the next, knit the 20 sleeve sts, pick up and knit another st from in between this st and the next, and then knit the remaining 8 cast-on sts. Join in the round, PM to mark the start of the round. You should now have 38 sts. Divide the sts evenly between the four needles.

Knit 3 rounds in stocking stitch and then begin the decreases.

Decrease round 1: k2tog, knit to the end of the round. *[1 st decreased]*

Knit 3 rounds in stocking stitch.

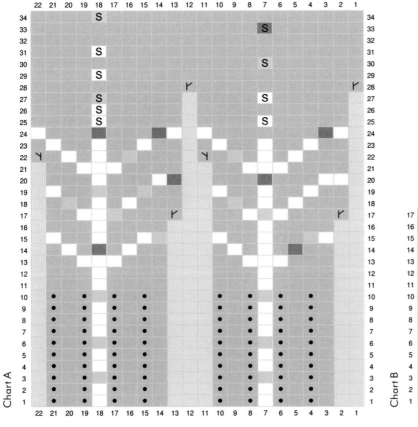

Chart A

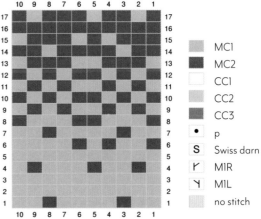

Chart B

MC1
MC2
CC1
CC2
CC3
•   p
S   Swiss darn
M1R
M1L
no stitch

Decrease round 2: Knit until 2 sts remain, k2tog.

[1 st decreased]

Knit 3 rounds in stocking stitch. Repeat the decrease round one more time. You should now have 35 sts. Continue knitting in stocking (stockinette) stitch until the sleeve is 6cm long. Knit chart D; the pattern will repeat 5 times per round. CC4 and CC5 are Swiss-darned onto the work afterwards. Knit all 26 rows of the chart and then cut the CCs and continue in MC2. Swap to 3.5mm (US 4) double-pointed needles and knit 1 round, decreasing 1 st. You should now have 34 sts. Work *k1, p1* ribbing for 2cm. Cast (bind) off using a stretchy cast-off method. Repeat for the other sleeve.

Finishing

Weave the ends into the wrong side of the work and gently wet the sweater in lukewarm water. Carefully squeeze out the excess water and shape the sweater. Leave to dry flat.

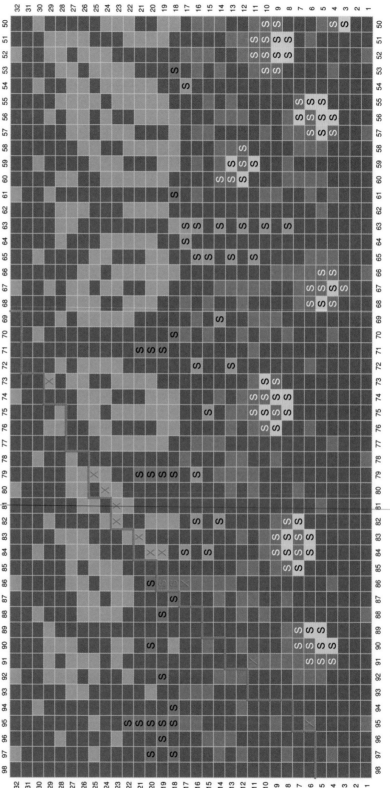

Chart C (Note that the chart is in two parts)

The larger dewdrops in the cobweb are not included on the neck of the dog version of the sweater so that they don't hinder your fur baby when exploring the bushes and undergrowth.

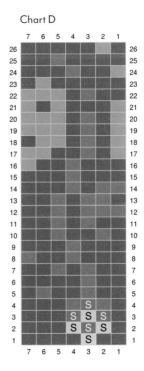

■ MC2
■ CC6
▨ CC5
■ CC4
■ CC7

S Swiss darn

S knit in MC2 for male dog version

X knit in MC2 for male dog version

☐ back of male dog sweater

Chart D

When I was coming up with a pattern, I thought about things that are specific to dogs. I didn't want to knit traditional pawprint or whisker patterns. What do dogs love? Sticks! Nothing is more fun than proudly carrying around a precious stick. And where do you find good sticks? In thickets, of course! I envisaged thickets and briar patches, and began to knit criss-crossing cables, without any set pattern in mind.

Risukko

ᐯ ᐯ ᐯ ᐯ ᐯ

ANNA-
KAROLIINA TETRI

www.tetridesign.com
FB Tetri Design
IG annakaroliinatetri

for humans

Shown in size XL

Sizes: XS (S, M, L) (XL, 2XL, 3XL, 4XL)

Recommended ease 5–10cm

∨∨∨∨∨∨∨∨∨∨∨∨∨∨∨∨∨∨∨∨∨∨∨∨∨∨∨∨∨∨∨∨

Measurements of finished sweater

Chest circumference: 82 (89, 100, 109)
(120, 131, 140, 151)cm

Length from armpit to hem: 47 (47, 48, 48)
(49, 50, 50, 50)cm

Front length, neck to hem: 73 (73, 74.5, 75)
(76.5, 78.5, 79.5, 80.5)cm

Upper sleeve circumference: 29 (31, 34.5, 36.5)
(40, 43.5, 45.5, 49)cm

Wrist circumference: 22 (22, 24.5, 24.5)
(26.5, 26.5, 29, 29)cm

Underarm sleeve length: 46 (47, 47, 48)
(49, 49, 51, 51)cm

∨∨∨∨∨∨∨∨∨∨∨∨∨∨∨∨∨∨∨∨∨∨∨∨∨∨∨∨∨∨∨∨

Yarn

Vuonue Kierrätys-Manta (70% Finnish sheep wool, 30% wool recycled in Finland; 180m/100g) and Manta villalanka (100% Finnish sheeps' wool; 180m/100g) or equivalent worsted weight yarn

MC: Harmaa 6 (7, 7, 7) (8, 8, 9, 9) hanks or 1080 (1260, 1260, 1260) (1440, 1440, 1620, 1620)m

CC: Tumma petrooli 2 (2, 2, 2) (2, 3, 3, 3) hanks or 360 (360, 360, 360) (360, 540, 540, 540)m

∨∨∨∨∨∨∨∨∨∨∨∨∨∨∨∨∨∨∨∨∨∨∨∨∨∨∨∨∨∨∨∨

Notions and tension (gauge)

Needles: 80–100cm circular needles in sizes 3.5mm (US 4) and 4.5mm (US 7) and, if necessary, double-pointed needles

You will also need: Stitch marker, stitch holders or spare yarn, tapestry needle

Tension: 18 sts and 23 rows = 10 × 10cm in stocking (stockinette) stitch on 4.5mm (US 7) needles and 22 sts and 23 rows = 10 x 10cm in cable knitting on 4.5mm (US 7) needles, lightly blocked. Knit a cable swatch as well as a stocking stitch swatch and adjust your needle size if necessary.

for dogs

Model: Segugio Italiano

One size

∨∨∨∨∨∨∨∨∨∨∨∨∨∨∨∨∨∨∨∨∨∨∨∨∨∨∨∨∨∨∨∨

Neck circumference: 46.5cm

Chest circumference: 74cm

Waist circumference: 60cm

Back length: 57.5cm (adjustable)

Vuonue Kierrätys-Manta (70% Finnish sheep wool, 30% wool recycled in Finland;180m/100g) and Manta villalanka (100% Finnish sheeps' wool; 180m/100g) or equivalent worsted weight yarn

MC: Sammalenvihreä 3 hanks or 540m

CC: Harmaa 1 hank or 180m

Needles: 40cm circular needles or double-pointed needles in size 3.5mm (US 4), two 60cm circular needles in size 4.5mm (US 7)

You will also need: Stitch marker, stitch holders or spare yarn, tapestry needle

Tension: 18 sts and 23 rows = 10 × 10cm in stocking stitch on 4.5mm (US 7) needles and 22 sts and 23 rows = 10 x 10cm in cable knitting on 4.5mm (US 7) needles, lightly blocked. Knit a cable swatch as well as a stocking stitch swatch and adjust your needle size if necessary.

Risukko for humans

Yoke

Using 3.5mm (US 4) circular needles, cast on 76 (80, 84, 84) (88, 88, 92, 96) sts in the MC. Join in the round, PM to mark the start of the round (centre back).

Work *k2, p2* ribbing for 16cm.

Sizes M–4XL only, next round (increase):

Size M: *k2, p2* 5 times, k1, M1, k1, *p2, k2* 5 times, M1P, *p2, k2* 5 times, p1, M1P, p1, *k2, p2* 5 times, M1P. [4 sts increased]

Size L: *k2, p2, k2, p1, M1P, p1, k2, p2, k2, M1P, p2, k2, p2, k1, M1, k1, p2, k2, p2, M1P*, repeat *–* 2 more times. [12 sts increased]

Size XL: *k2, p2, M1P, k2, p2, k2, M1P, p2, k2, p2, M1P, k2, p2, k2, M1P, p2, k2, M1P, p2, k2, p2, M1P, k2, p2, k2, M1P, p2, k2, p2, M1P*, repeat *–* one more time. [16 sts increased]

Size 2XL: **Knit *k2, p2, M1P* twice, k2, p1, M1P, p1, k2, M1P, *p2, k2, M1P* 4 times, p2, k1, M1, k1, p2, M1P, *k2, p2, M1P* twice**, repeat **–** one more time. [24 sts increased]

Size 3XL: k2, p2, *k2, p1, M1P, p1, k2, M1P, p2, k1, M1, k1, p2, M1P*, repeat *–* 6 more times, k2, p2. [28 sts increased]

Size 4XL: *k2, p1, M1P, p1, k2, M1P, p2, k1, M1, k1, p2, M1P*, repeat *–* 7 more times. [32 sts increased]

You should now have 76 (80, 88, 96) (104, 112, 120, 128) sts.

Swap to 4.5mm (US 7) needles. Continue to knit/purl in stocking (stockinette) stitch in the CC.

Raise the neck with short rows as follows:

(always work DSs as single sts).

Row 1 (RS): p8 (9, 10, 11) (12, 13, 14, 15), turn.

Row 2 (WS): DS, knit to round marker, SM, k8 (9, 10, 11) (12, 13, 14, 15), turn.

Row 3 (RS): DS, purl to round marker, SM, p17 (18, 20, 22) (23, 25, 27, 29), turn.

Row 4 (WS): DS, knit to round marker, SM, k17 (18, 20, 22) (23, 25, 27, 29), turn.

Row 5 (RS): DS, purl to round marker, SM, p25 (26, 29, 31) (34, 36, 39, 42), turn.

Row 6 (WS): DS, knit to round marker, SM, k25 (26, 29, 31) (34, 36, 39, 42), turn.

Row 7 (RS): DS, knit to round marker, SM.

Knit 0 (0, 1, 2) (3, 6, 8, 10) rounds of reverse stocking stitch.

Next round (increase): *p2, M1P*, repeat *–* until the end of the round. You should now have 114 (120, 132, 144) (156, 168, 180, 192) sts.

Now knit the chart. The pattern repeats 19 (20, 22, 24) (26, 28, 30, 32) times per round. In some places, the cables cross over rounds. For cables that cross over from one round to the next, do not knit the first sts in the round; knit them into the cabling at the end of the round. Keep the round marker where it is. Knit all 60 rows of the chart and then cut the CC and continue in the MC. You should now have 228 (240, 264, 288) (312, 336, 360, 384) sts. Knit 1 round in stocking stitch in the MC.

Body

The body is knitted in stocking stitch in the MC.

Next round: RM, knit the 34 (36, 40, 44) (48, 52, 56, 60) back sts, place 46 (48, 52, 56) (60, 64, 68, 72) sleeve sts onto a stitch holder, cast on 3 (4, 5, 5) (6, 7, 7, 8) armpit sts, PM (this is the new round marker), cast on 3 (4, 5, 5) (6, 7, 7, 8) sts, knit the 68 (72, 80, 88) (96, 104, 112, 120) front sts, place 46 (48, 52, 56) (60, 64, 68, 72) sleeve sts onto a stitch holder, cast on 6 (8, 10, 10) (12, 14, 14, 16) armpit sts, knit to the end of the round. You should now have 148 (160, 180, 196) (216, 236, 252, 272) sts.

Continue in stocking stitch in the MC until the work measures 41 (41, 42, 42) (43, 44, 44, 44)cm from the armpit.

Swap to 3.5mm (US 4) needles and work *k2, p2* ribbing for 6cm.

Cast (bind) off using a stretchy cast-off method.

Chart column numbers (top): 18 17 16 15 14 13 12 11 10 9 8 7 6 5 4 3 2 1

Chart row numbers (right side): 60 59 58 57 56 55 54 53 52 51 50 49 48 47 46 45 44 43 42 41 40 39 38 37 36 35 34 33 32 31 30 29 28 27 26 25 24 23 22 21 20 19 18 17 16 15 14 13 12 11 10 9 8 7 6 5 4 3 2 1

Chart column numbers (bottom): 18 17 16 15 14 13 12 11 10 9 8 7 6 5 4 3 2 1

Risukko is knitted top-down in the round.

Sleeves

Move the sleeve sts from the stitch holder onto 4.5mm (US 7) needles. Starting from the middle of the armpit and working in the MC, pick up and knit 3 (4, 5, 5) (6, 7, 7, 8) sts, knit the 46 (48, 52, 56) (60, 64, 68 72) sleeve sts, pick up and knit 3 (4, 5, 5) (6, 7, 7, 8) sts, PM. You should now have 52 (56, 62, 66) (72, 78, 82, 88) sts.

Knit 12cm in stocking stitch.

Next round (decrease): k2, k2tog, knit until 4 sts remain, ssk, k2. *[2 sts decreased]*

Repeat the decrease row every 10th (8th, 7th, 6th) (5th, 4th, 4th, 4th) round another 5 (7, 8, 10) (11, 14, 14, 17) times.

You should now have 40 (40, 44, 44) (48, 48, 52, 52) sts.

Continue in stocking stitch until the sleeve is 40 (41, 41, 42) (43, 43, 45, 45)cm long.

Swap to 3.5mm (US 4) needles and work 6cm of *k2, p2* ribbing.

Cast off using a stretchy cast-off method.

Repeat for the other sleeve.

Finishing

Sew in the ends. Dampen the sweater, shape it, and then leave to dry flat.

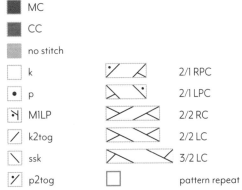

- ■ MC
- ■ CC
- ■ no stitch

☐ k	⟋·⟍ 2/1 RPC
• p	⟍ ⟋· 2/1 LPC
M1LP	⟋⟍ 2/2 RC
⟋ k2tog	⟍⟋ 2/2 LC
⟍ ssk	⟍⟋ 3/2 LC
⟋ p2tog	☐ pattern repeat

The dog's sweater is knitted in two parts from the neck down. The body will continue from the yoke and is knitted flat at first, then in the round at the belly, and flat again at the hem. The chest panel that combines the yoke and body is knitted separately to a suitable length. The length of the collar and body can be adjusted to your dog's own measurements. This pattern is suitable for both male and female dogs.

The Risukko sweater is designed to keep large and active short-haired breeds warm on cool days. The Segugio Italiano is a hunting dog that requires a loose fit and room for leg movement. The sleeveless sweater covers the back and large muscles.

Risukko for dogs

Neck

Using 3.5mm (US 4) circular needles, cast on 84 sts in the CC. Join in the round, PM to mark the start of the round (centre neck).

Work 9cm of *k2, p2* ribbing.

Note: The neck is folded double. If you wish, you can knit a shorter ribbed collar.

On the last round of ribbing, increase 3 sts spaced at regular intervals. You should now have 87 sts.

Swap to 4.5mm (US 7) needles. Knit 1 round in the CC.

Next round (increase): p8, *(M1P, p4) 6 times, M1P*, repeat *–* twice more, p7. You should now have 108 sts.

Yoke

Begin to knit the chart. The pattern repeats 9 times in each round. In some places, the cables cross over rounds. For cables that cross over from one round to the next, do not knit the first sts in the round; knit them into the cabling at the end of the round. Keep the round marker where it is. Knit all 35 rows of the chart and then cut the CC and continue in the MC. Knit 1 round. You should now have 117 sts.

The circumference of the work at this point is around 65cm, and the edge should come to just above the front legs when tried on. If necessary, knit a few additional rounds.

Body

The body is initially knitted in rows in stocking (stockinette) stitch with ribbing at the edges.

Next row (RS): k34, p2, k2, p2, k3, p1.

For the left shoulder pleat, pick up the 4 sts underneath the 4 sts you last knitted, and move them to the left-hand needle [4 sts increased]. Turn.

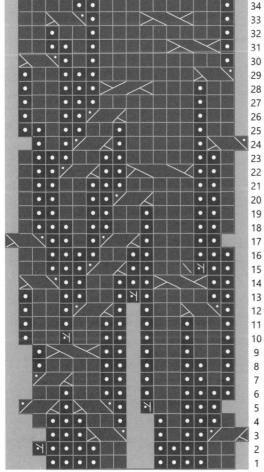

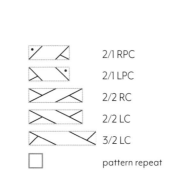

■ MC	
■ CC	
■ no stitch	▪╱ ╲▪ 2/1 RPC
□ k	╲ ╱▪ 2/1 LPC
• p	⟩╱ 2/2 RC
↘ M1LP	╲⟨ 2/2 LC
╱ k2tog	╲⟨ 3/2 LC
╲ ssk	□ pattern repeat

Next row (WS): p4, k2, p2, k2, p68, k2, p2, k2, p4.

For the right shoulder pleat, where the back piece remains uppermost, pick up the 4 sts underneath the 4 sts you last knitted with the left-hand needle *[4 sts increased]*.

Place the next 37 sts (4+29+4 sts) from the left needle onto a stitch holder until you are ready to knit the chest. Continue knitting the body.

Row 1 (RS): p1, k3, p2, k2, p2, M1R, knit until 10 sts remain, M1L, p2, k2, p2, k3, p1. *[2 sts increased]*

Row 2 (WS): p4, k2, p2, k2, knit until 10 sts remain, k2, p2, k2, p4.

Repeat rows 1–2 another 4 times.

Row 11 (RS): p1, k3, p2, k2, p2, M1R, knit until 10 sts remain, M1L, p2, k2, p2, k3, p1. *[2 sts increased]*

Row 12 (WS): p4, k2, p2, k2, knit until 10 sts remain, k2, p2, k2, p4.

Row 13 (RS): p1, k3, p2, k2, p2, knit until 10 sts remain, p2, k2, p2, k3, p1.

Row 14: As for row 12.

Repeat rows 11–14 twice more.

Row 23 (RS): p1, k3, p2, k2, p2, M1R, knit until 10 sts remain, M1L, p2, k2, p2, k3, p1. *[2 sts increased]*

Row 24 (WS): p4, k2, p2, k2, purl until 10 sts remain, k2, p2, k2, p4

Row 25 (RS): p1, k3, p2, k2, p2, knit until 10 sts remain, p2, k2, p2, k3, p1.

Row 26: As for row 24.

Row 27: As for row 25.

Row 28: As for row 24.

Repeat rows 23–25 one more time and then check to see if the back is a suitable length (the sample shown on the model is 13.5cm long).

You should now have 108 sts. The yarn should be to the left edge. Leave these sts on the circular needles.

Knit the chest strip, which will be joined to the body later.

Note: The length of the back and chest can be adjusted to your dog's measurements. The holes for the front legs can be spacious to allow sufficient room for movement.

Chest

The chest is knitted flat in stocking (stockinette) stitch with ribbing on the edges to match the back.

Place the 37 sts from the stitch holder onto 4.5mm (US 7) needles. Swap to the CC.

Row 1 (RS, decrease): p1, k3, p2, k2, p2, *ssk, k3* twice, k2tog, k3, k2tog, p2, k2, p2, k3, p1. *[4 sts decreased]*

Row 2 (WS): p4, k2, p2, k2, knit until 10 sts remain, k2, p2, k2, p4.

Row 3 (RS): p1, k3, p2, k2, p2, knit until 10 sts remain, p2, k2, p2, k3, p1.

Row 4: As for row 2.

Row 5 (RS, decrease): p1, k3, p2, k2, p2, k3, ssk, k3, k2tog, k3, p2, k2, p2, k3, p1. *[2 sts decreased]*

Row 6: As for row 2.

Row 7: As for row 3.

Row 8: As for row 2.

Repeat rows 7–8 one more time.

Row 11 (RS, decrease): p1, k3, p2, k2, p2, k2, ssk, k3, k2tog, k2, p2, k2, p2, k3, p1. *[2 sts decreased]*

Row 12: As for row 2.

Row 13: As for row 3.

Row 14: As for row 2.

Repeat rows 13–14 one more time.

Row 17 (RS, decrease): p1, k3, p2, k2, p2, k1, ssk, k3, k2tog, k1, p2, k2, p2, k3, p1. *[2 sts decreased]*

Row 18: As for row 2.

Row 19: As for row 3.

Row 20: As for row 2.

Repeat rows 19–20 one more time.

Row 23 (RS decrease): p1, k3, p2, k2, p2, ssk, k3, k2tog, p2, k2, p2, k3, p1. *[2 sts decreased]*

You should now have 25 sts.

Row 24: As for row 2.

Row 25: As for row 3.

Row 26: As for row 2.

Repeat rows 25–26 another 3 times.

The piece should now measure 14cm.

Begin the increases as follows:

Row 1 (increase, RS): p1, k3, p2, k2, p2, M1R, knit until 10 sts remain, M1L, p2, k2, p2, k3, p1. *[2 sts increased]*

Row 2 (WS): p4, k2, p2, k2, purl until 10 sts remain, k2, p2, k2, p4.

Row 3 (RS): p1, k3, p2, k2, p2, knit until 10 sts remain, p2, k2, p2, k3, p1.

Row 4: As for row 2.

Row 5: As for row 3.

Row 6: As for row 2.

Row 7: As for row 3.

Row 8: As for row 2.

Repeat rows 1–8 another 3 times or until the length of the chest panel is suitable (the sample shown on the model is 28cm long). You should now have 33 sts. Cut the CC.

Combine the body and the chest:

Using a cable needle and in the CC, pick up the last 4 purl sts underneath the last four sts on the edge of the body and knit them together with the first four knit sts on the chest using the three-needle cast-off (bind-off) technique. Cut the CC and continue knitting with the remaining MC on the back.

Continue with the chest sts: Move the stitch leftover from joining to the left needle, p2tog, p1, k2, p2, k13, p2, k2, p2 (4 sts remain).

From the other edge of the body and using a cable needle, pick up 4 purl sts from underneath the first four sts and knit them together with the last four knit sts on the chest using the three-needle cast-off technique. Slip the first 4 sts of the body onto the right needle, lift the stitch that was leftover from joining onto the left needle, p2tog, k3, p2, k2, p2, knit to SM. You should now have 133 sts.

Next round: k44, p2, k2, p2, *k3, p3, k2, p2, k2, p3* twice, k3, p2, k2, p2, k44.

Continue as set until the work measures 15cm after joining, or until the belly side is a suitable length (remember to leave enough room for male dogs to pee).

Next round: k44, p2, k2, p2, k3, p1, cast off the next 25 sts, p1, k3, p2, k2, p2, k44, RM, knit until 10 sts remain, p2, k2, p2, k3, p1.

Now work in rows.

Row 1 (WS): p4, k2, p2, k2, purl until 10 sts remain, k2, p2, k2, p4.

Row 2 (RS, decrease): p1, k3, p2, k2, p2, ssk, knit until 12 sts remain, k2tog, p2, k2, p2, k3, p1. *[2 sts decreased]*

Row 3: As for row 1.

Row 4: p1, k3, p2, k2, p2, knit until 10 sts remain, p2, k2, p2, k3, p1.

Repeat rows 1–4 another 7 times and then repeat rows 1–3 once more. You should now have 90 sts and have knitted approx. 15cm. The work should reach to about the front of the hind legs.

Shape the rear using short rows:

Row 1 (RS): p1, k3, p2, k2, p2, k62, PM, k8, p2, k2, p2, k3, p1.

Row 2 (WS): p4, k2, p2, k2, purl to marker, turn.

Row 3 (RS): DS, knit until 10 sts remain, p2, k2, p2, k3, p1.

Row 4 (WS): p4, k2, p2, k2, purl to marker, RM, purl until 18 sts remain, PM, p8, k2, p2, k2, p4.

Row 5 (RS): p1, k3, p2, k2, p2, knit to marker, turn.

Row 6 (WS): DS, purl until 10 sts remain, k2, p2, k2, p4.

Row 7 (RS): p1, k3, p2, k2, p2, knit to marker, RM, knit until 24 sts remain, PM, knit until 10 sts remain, p2, k2, p2, k3, p1.

Row 8: As for row 2.

Row 9: As for row 3.

Row 10 (WS): p4, k2, p2, k2, purl to marker, RM, purl until 24 sts remain, PM, purl until 10 sts remain, p4, k2, p2, k2, p4.

Row 11: As for row 5.

Row 12: As for row 6.

Row 13: p1, k3, p2, k2, p2, knit to marker, RM, knit until 30 sts remain, PM, k20, p2, k2, p2, k3, p1.

Row 14: As for row 2.

Row 15: As for row 3.

Row 16 (WS): p4, k2, p2, k2, purl to marker, RM, purl until 30 sts remain, PM, purl until 10 sts remain, k2, p2, k2, p4.

Row 17 (RS): As for row 5.

Row 18: As for row 6.

Row 19: As for row 7.

Row 20: As for row 2.

Row 21: As for row 3.

Row 22: As for row 10.

Row 23: As for row 5.

Row 24: As for row 6.

Row 25: As for row 1.

Row 26: As for row 2.

Row 27: As for row 3.

Row 28: As for row 4.

Row 29: As for row 5.

Row 30: As for row 6.

Begin the decreases:

Row 1 (RS): p1, k3, p2, k2, p2, ssk, knit to marker, RM, knit until 12 sts remain, k2tog, p2, k2, p2, k3, p1. *[2 sts decreased]*

Row 2 (WS): p4, k2, p2, k2, purl until 10 sts remain, k2, p2, k2, p4.

Row 3 (RS): p1, k3, p2, k2, p2, ssk, knit until 12 sts remain, k2tog, p2, k2, p2, k3, p1. *[2 sts decreased]*

Row 4: As for row 2.

Repeat rows 3–4 three more times. You should now have 80 sts.

Row 11 (RS): p1, k3, p2, k2, p2, ssk, k26, ssk, k4, k2tog, knit until 12 sts remain, k2tog, p2, k2, p2, k3, p1. *[4 sts decreased]*

Row 12: As for row 2.

Row 13 (RS): p1, k3, p2, k2, p2, ssk, k24, ssk, k4, k2tog, knit until 12 sts remain, k2tog, p2, k2, p2, k3, p1. *[4 sts decreased]*

Row 14: As for row 2.

Row 15 (RS): p1, k3, p2, k2, p2, ssk, knit until 12 sts remain, k2tog, p2, k2, p2, k3, p1. *[2 sts decreased]*

Next row (WS): p4, k2, *p2, k2*, repeat *–*, until 4 sts remain, p4.

Next row (RS): p1, k3, p2 *k2, p2*, repeat *–*, until 4 sts remain, k3, p1.

Repeat these two rows for 4cm.

Cast (bind) off.

Finishing

Weave in the ends and lightly steam the work.

If the hem of the sweater flaps around too much, add some cords that run under the hind legs to keep it in place. You can knit an i-cord 2cm wide, or use thick elasticated cord. Measure the length for the cords from the side of the hem to the back corner behind the dog's hind leg, not forgetting to account for room for movement. Sew one end of the cord to the sweater and attach a suspender clip to the other end to make the sweater easier to put on.

Semper in corde meo

The back of this sweater reads 'Forever in my heart'. And animal friends do, indeed, leave eternal pawprints on your heart. I hope I can always be the great person my dogs believe me to be (fat chance!).

ᐯᐯᐯᐯᐯ

MARJUKKA VUORISALO
FB risaineri
RAVELRY
Marjukka Vuorisalo

for humans

Shown in size XL
Sizes: XS (S, M, L) (XL, 2XL, 3XL, 4XL)
Recommended ease 2cm

vvvvvvvvvvvvvvvvvvvvvvvvvvvvvvvvvvvv

Measurements of finished sweater
Chest circumference: 70 (79, 90, 101)
(110, 121, 130, 141)cm
Length from armpit to hem: 46.5 (46, 46, 45.5)
(45.5, 44.5, 44.5, 44)cm
Front length, neck to hem: 62.5cm (all sizes)
Upper sleeve circumference: 32.5 (34.5, 36.5, 38)
(41, 42.5, 44.5, 46.5)cm
Wrist circumference: 19 (19, 20, 20) (21, 21, 26.5, 26.5)cm
Underarm sleeve length: 49 (50, 51.5, 52)
(54, 55, 55, 56.5)cm

vvvvvvvvvvvvvvvvvvvvvvvvvvvvvvvvvvvv

Yarn
*Lankava Lysti (75% superwash wool, 25% polyamide;
200m/100g) and Taito Shop Olli (75% wool, 25%
polyamide; 200m/100g) or equivalent Aran weight yarn*
MC: Lysti 855 Salmiakki 7 (7, 7, 8) (8, 8, 9, 9) skeins or
1400 (1400, 1400, 1600) (1600, 1600, 1800, 1800)m
CC1: Lysti 852 Usva 3 (3, 3, 3) (3, 3, 3, 3) skeins or 600
(600, 600, 600) (600, 600, 600, 600)m
CC2: Lysti 860 Pesto 1 (1, 1, 1) (1, 1, 1, 1) skein or 200
(200, 200, 200) (200, 200, 200, 200)m
CC3: Olli 4267 Punainen 1 (1, 1, 1) (1, 1, 1, 1) skein or 200
(200, 200, 200) (200, 200, 200, 200)m

vvvvvvvvvvvvvvvvvvvvvvvvvvvvvvvvvvvv

Notions and tension (gauge)
Needles: 80–100cm circular needles in sizes 3.5mm (US 4)
and 4mm (US 6)
You will also need: Stitch markers, stitch holders or spare
yarn, tapestry needle
Tension: 22 sts and 32 rows = 10 x 10cm in stocking
(stockinette) stitch on 4mm (US 6) needles, lightly blocked.
Knit a swatch in colourwork and adjust your needle size
if necessary.

for dogs

Dog model (male, size 2)
Sizes: 1 (2, 3)

Measurements of finished sweater
Neck circumference: 34 (39.5, 71.5)cm
Chest circumference: 61 (74.5, 111)cm
Waist circumference: 34.5 (40, 77.5)cm
Back length: 36.5 (59, 77)cm
Sleeve circumference at top: 19.5 (17.5, 29)cm
Sleeve circumference at bottom: 14 (12, 21)cm
Sleeve length: 14 (25, 36.5)cm

Yarn
*Lankava Lysti (75% superwash wool, 25% polyamide;
200m/100g) and Taito Shop Olli (75% wool, 25%
polyamide; 200m/100g) or equivalent Aran weight yarn*
MC: Lysti 855 Salmiakki 3 (4, 5) skeins or 600
(800, 1000)m
CC1: Lysti 852 Usva 2 (2, 2) skeins or 400 (400, 400)m
CC2: Lysti 860 Pesto 1 (1, 1) skein or 200 (200, 200)m
CC3: Olli 4267 Punainen 1 (1, 1) skein or 200 (200, 200)m

Notions and tension (gauge)
Needles: 80–100cm circular needles in sizes 3.5mm (US 4)
and 4mm (US 6)
You will also need: Stitch markers, stitch holder or spare
yarn, tapestry needle
Tension: 22 sts and 32 rows = 10 x 10cm in stocking stitch
on 4mm (US 6) needles, lightly blocked. Knit a swatch in
colourwork and adjust your needle size if necessary.

TIP

You can change the text in the ribbon on the back of the sweater to something different and meaningful to you and your dog. The pattern contains a blank ribbon and lettering charts for this purpose.

Semper in corde meo for humans

Front

Using 3.5mm (US 4) needles, cast on 79 (89, 101, 113) (123, 135, 145, 157) sts in the MC.

Sizes XS, XL and 2XL only:

Row 1 (RS): k1, p2, *k2, p2* to the end of the row.

Row 2 (WS): *k2, p2*, repeat *–* until 3 sts remain, k2, p1.

Sizes S, M, L, 3XL and 4XL only:

Row 1 (RS): k1, *p2, k2* to the end of the row.

Row 2 (WS): *p2, k2*, repeat *–* until 1 st remains, p1.

All sizes:

Repeat rows 1 and 2 until you have 5cm of ribbing. Swap to 4mm (US 6) needles and work in stocking (stockinette) stitch using the MC for 114 (112, 110, 108) (106, 100, 96, 92) rows.

Next row (RS, decrease): Cast (bind) off 2 sts, knit to end of row.

Next row (WS, decrease): Cast off 2 sts, purl to end of row.

Repeat these 2 rows twice more. You should now have 67 (77, 89, 101) (111, 123, 133, 145) sts.

Continue to work in stocking stitch until you have knitted row 154.

Next row (RS): k14 (19, 25, 31) (36, 42, 47, 53), cast off 39 sts.

Set aside the sts for the right-front section and first knit the left-front section.

Left-front section:

Row 1 (WS): Cast off 2 sts, purl to the end of the row.

Row 2 (RS): Knit to the end of the row.

Repeat rows 1 and 2 twice more. You should now have 8 (13, 19, 25) (30, 36, 41, 47) sts.

Work another 23 rows in stocking stitch. Cast off the shoulder sts.

Right-front section:

Work the right-front sts that you set aside and begin in the MC from the edge of the neck.

Row 1 (RS): Cast off 2 sts, knit to the end of the row.

Row 2 (WS): Purl to the end of the row.

Repeat rows 1 and 2 twice more. You should now have 8 (13, 19, 25) (30, 36, 41, 47) sts.

Knit another 24 rows in stocking stitch. Cast off the shoulder sts.

Now knit the neck:

Using 3.5mm (US 4) needles, pick up 79 sts from the neck in the MC.

Row 1 (RS): k1, p2, *k2, p2* to the end of the row.

Row 2 (WS): *k2, p2*, repeat *–* until 3 sts remain, k2, p1.

Repeat rows 1 and 2 until you have 5cm of ribbing. Cast off the sts.

Back

Using 3.5mm (US 4) needles, cast on 79 (89, 101, 113) (123, 135, 145, 157) sts in the MC.

Sizes XS, XL and 2XL only:

Row 1 (RS): k1, p2, *k2, p2* to the end of the row.

Row 2 (WS): *k2, p2*, repeat *–* until 3 sts remain, k2, p1.

Sizes S, M, L, 3XL and 4XL only:

Row 1 (RS): k1, *p2, k2* to the end of the row.

Row 2 (WS): *k2, p2*, repeat *–* until 1 st remains, p1.

All sizes:

Repeat rows 1 and 2 until you have 5cm of ribbing. Swap to 4mm (US 6) needles and begin the colourwork following the chart on pages 74–75:

Row 1 (RS): In the MC, k1 (6, 12, 18) (23, 29, 34, 40), PM, work row 1 of the chart, PM, knit to the end of the row in the MC.

Row 2 (WS): Purl to the marker in the MC, SM, work the next row of the chart, SM, purl to the end of the row in the MC.

Row 3 (RS): Knit to the marker in the MC, SM, work the next row of the chart, SM, knit to the end of the row in the MC.

Row 4 (WS): Purl to the marker in the MC, SM, work the next row of the chart, SM, purl to the end of the row in the MC.

Repeat rows 3 and 4 until you have knitted row 114 (112, 110, 108) (106, 100, 96, 92) of the chart.

Next row (RS, decrease): Cast off 2 sts, knit to the marker in the MC, SM, work the next row of the chart, SM, knit to the end of the row in the MC.

Next row (WS, decrease): Cast off 2 sts, purl to the marker in the MC, SM, work the next row of the chart, SM, purl to the end of the row.

Repeat these 2 rows twice more. You should now have 67 (77, 89, 101) (111, 123, 133, 145) sts.

Next round: Knit to the marker in the MC, SM, work the next row of the chart, SM, knit to the end of the row in the MC.

Next row: Purl to the marker in the MC, SM, work the next row of the chart, SM, purl to the end of the row in the MC. Repeat these last two rows until you have knitted all 165 rows of the chart. Cut the CCs and continue in the MC.

Next row (WS): Purl to the end of the row (removing the markers as you go).

Next row (RS): k14 (19, 25, 31) (36, 42, 47, 53), cast off 39 sts.

Set aside the sts for the left-back section and first knit the right-back section.

Right-back section:

Row 1 (WS): Cast off 2 sts, purl to the end of the row.

Row 2 (RS): Knit to the end of the row.

Repeat rows 1 and 2 twice more. You should now have 8 (13, 19, 25) (30, 36, 41, 47) sts.

Cast off the shoulder sts.

Left-back section:

Work the left-back sts that you set aside and begin in the MC from the edge of the neck.

Row 1 (RS): Cast off 2 sts, knit to the end of the row.

Row 2 (WS): Purl to the end of the row.

Repeat rows 1 and 2 twice more. You should now have 8 (13, 19, 25) (30, 36, 41, 47) sts.

Knit one more row. Cast off the shoulder sts.

Now knit the neck:

Using 3.5mm (US 4) needles, pick up 47 sts from the neck in the MC.

Row 1 (RS): k1, p2, *k2, p2* to the end of the row.

Row 2 (WS): *k2, p2*, repeat *–* until 3 sts remain, k2, p1.

Repeat rows 1 and 2 until you have 5cm of ribbing. Cast off the sts.

Sleeves

Using 3.5mm (US 4) needles, cast on 42 (42, 44, 44) (46, 46, 58, 58) sts in the MC.

Sizes XS, S, XL, 2XL, 3XL and 4XL only:

Row 1 (RS): k2, *p2, k2* to the end of the row.

Row 2 (WS): *p2, k2*, repeat *–* until 2 sts remain, p2.

Sizes M and L only:

Row 1 (RS): *k2, p2* to the end of the row.

Row 2 (WS): *k2, p2* to the end of the row.

All sizes:

Repeat rows 1 and 2 until you have 5cm of ribbing. Swap to 4mm (US 6) needles and continue to work in stocking stitch using the MC. Begin sleeve increases immediately.

Increase row (RS): K1, M1R, knit until 1 st remains, M1L, k1.

[2 sts increased]

Chart for the human version of the sweater (Note that the chart is in two parts)

MC

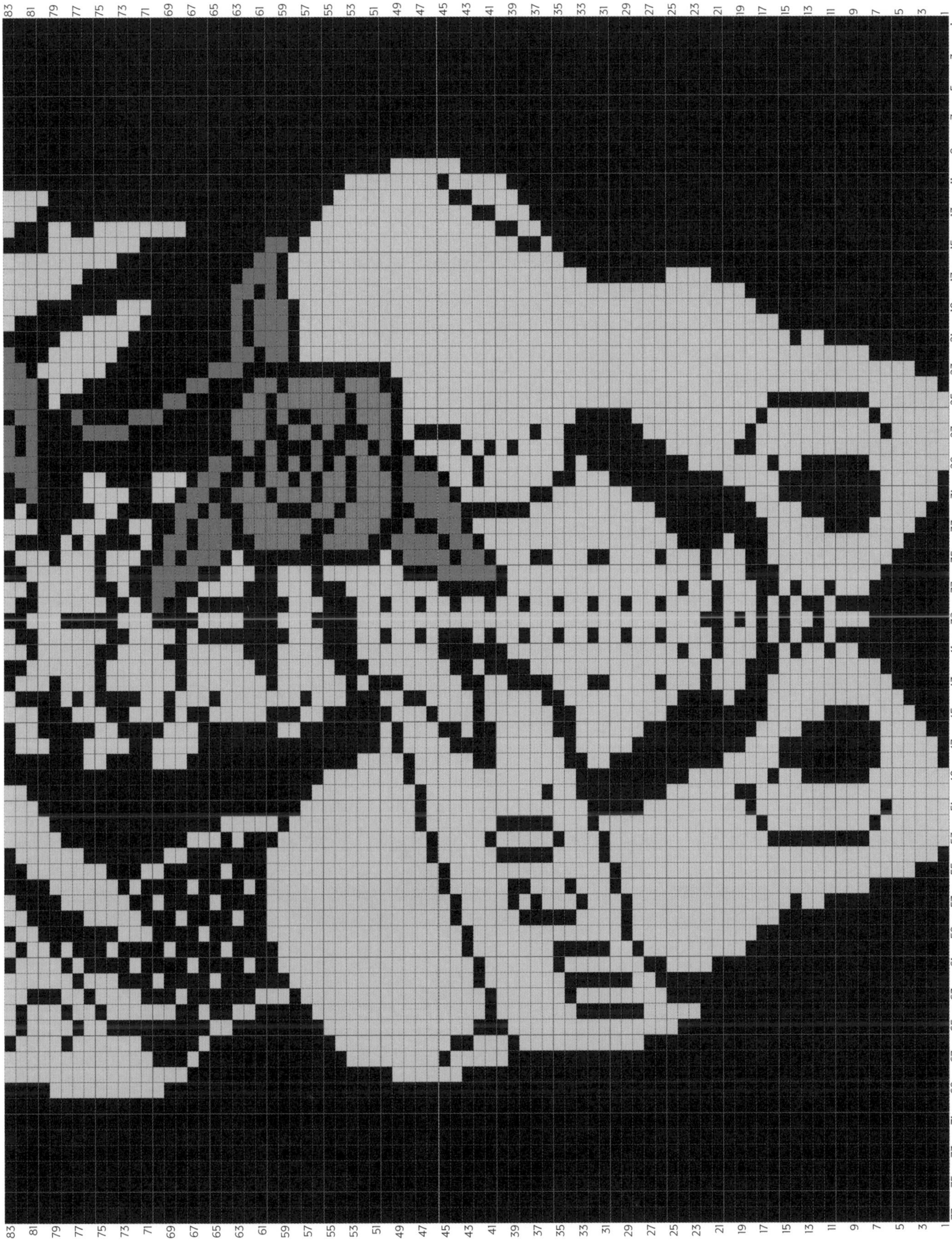

CC3

Repeat the increase row another 14 (16, 17, 19) (21, 23, 19, 21) times every 9th (8th, 8th, 7th) (7th, 6th, 8th, 7th) row. **Note:** When increasing on WS rows, purl the increases. You should now have 72 (76, 80, 84) (90, 94, 98, 102) sts. Work another 13 (15, 11, 16) (8, 21, 7, 16) rows in stocking (stockinette) stitch.

Begin the decreases for the sleeve yoke:

Row 1 (RS): Cast (bind) off 6 sts, knit to end of row.

Row 2 (WS): Cast off 6 sts, purl to end of row.

Row 3: Cast off 4 sts, knit to end of row.

Round 4: Cast off 4 sts, purl to end of row.

Row 5: Cast off 3 sts, knit to end of row.

Row 6: Cast off 3 sts, purl to end of row.

Repeat rows 5 and 6 one more time.

Row 9: Cast off 2 sts, knit to end of row.

Row 10: Cast off 2 sts, purl to end of row.

Repeat rows 9 and 10 one more time.

Row 13: Cast off 1 st, knit to end of row.

Row 14: Cast off 1 st, purl to end of row.

Repeat rows 13 and 14 one more time. You should now have 28 (32, 36, 40) (46, 50, 54, 58) sts.

Knit another 0 (2, 2, 4) (4, 6, 6, 8) rows in stocking stitch. Now knit the following decreases.

Row 1 (RS): Cast off 1 st, knit to end of row.

Row 2 (WS): Cast off 1 st, purl to end of row.

Repeat rows 1 and 2 another 3 times.

Row 9: Cast off 2 sts, knit to end of row.

Row 10: Cast off 2 sts, purl to end of row.

Row 11: Cast off 3 sts, knit to end of row.

Row 12: Cast off 3 sts, purl to end of row.

You should now have 10 (14, 18, 22) (28, 32, 36, 40) sts. Cast off.

Repeat for the other sleeve.

Finishing

Lightly steam the pieces. Sew the shoulder seams, side seams and vertical sleeve seams. Attach the sleeves. Tidy up the ends.

Start on a matching sweater for your doggy companion!

TIP

∨ ∨ ∨ ∨ ∨

Find the charts for a blank ribbon and lettering on pages 82–83 for the human sweater and on pages 84–85 for the dog version.

Semper in corde meo **for dogs**

Back panel

Using 3.5mm (US 4) needles, cast on 77 (89, 159) sts in the MC.

Sizes 1 and 2 only:

Row 1 (RS): k1, repeat *p2, k2* to the end of the row.

Row 2 (WS): Repeat *p2, k2*, repeat *-* until 1 st remains, p1.

Size 3 only:

Row 1 (RS): k1, p2, repeat *k2, p2* to the end of the row.

Row 2 (WS): Repeat *k2, p2*, repeat *-* until 3 sts remain, k2, p1.

All sizes:

Repeat rows 1 and 2 until you have 5cm of ribbing.

Swap to 4mm (US 6) needles and begin colourwork following the chart on pages 80–81.

Note: The chart has 175 rows. For size 3 you will work the full chart but sizes 1 and 2 will be shorter than this. For size 3, knit to the end of the chart and then continue in the MC for the remaining rows.

Row 1 (RS): In the MC, k12 (18, 53), PM, knit row 1 of the chart, PM, knit to the end of the row in the MC.

Row 2 (WS): Purl to the marker in the MC, SM, work the next row of the chart, SM, purl to the end of the row in the MC.

Row 3 (RS, increase): In the MC, k1, M1R, knit to marker, SM, work the next row of the chart, SM, knit in the MC until 1 st remains, M1L, k1. *[2 sts increased]*

Row 4 (WS): Purl to the marker in the MC, SM, work the next row of the chart, SM, purl to the end of the row in the MC.

Repeat rows 3 and 4 another 18 (25, 28) times. You should now have 115 (141, 217) sts.

Next row (RS): Knit to the marker in the MC, SM, knit the next row of the chart, SM, knit to the end of the row in the MC.

Next row (WS): Purl to the marker in the MC, SM, work the next row of the chart, SM, purl to the end of the row in the MC.

Repeat these two rows until you have knitted row 54 (100, 150) of the chart.

Begin the decreases:

Decrease row (RS): In the MC, k1, k2tog, knit to marker, SM, knit the next row of the chart, SM, knit in the MC until 3 sts remain, ssk, k1. *[2 sts decreased]*

Repeat the decrease row every 4th (4th, 4th) row another 5 (14, 13) times. You should now have 103 (111, 189) sts.

Now knit the pattern without decreases for 10 (0, 12) rows.

Begin the cast (bind) off:

Row 1 (RS): Cast off 2 sts, knit to the marker in the MC, SM, work the next row of the chart, SM, knit to the end of the row in the MC.

Row 2 (WS): Cast off 2 sts, purl to the marker in the MC, SM, work the next row of the chart, SM, purl to the end of the row in the MC.

Repeat rows 1 and 2 twice more.

Row 7: Cast off 3 sts, knit to the marker in the MC, SM, work the next row of the chart, SM, knit to the end of the row in the MC.

Row 8: Cast off 3 sts, purl to the marker in the MC, SM, work the next row of the chart, SM, purl to the end of the row in the MC.

Repeat rows 7 and 8 twice more.

Row 13: Cast off 4 sts, knit to the marker in the MC, SM, work the next row of the chart, SM, knit to the end of the row in the MC.

Row 14: Cast off 4 sts, purl to the marker in the MC, SM, work the next row of the chart, SM, purl to the end of the row in the MC.

Repeat rows 13 and 14 one more time.

Cast off the remaining 57 (65, 143) sts.

Belly panel

Using 4mm (US 6) needles cast on 3 sts in the MC. The belly panel is worked in stocking (stockinette) stitch. Begin the increases immediately in the first row.

Increase row (RS): k1, M1R, knit until 1 st remains, M1L, k1. *[2 sts increased]*

Repeat the increase row every 3rd (5th, 8th) row another 9 (11, 13) times.

Note: When increasing on a WS row, purl the increases. You should now have 23 (27, 31) sts.

Continue in stocking stitch without increases for another 66 (48, 137) rows (or, for male dogs, until the belly is 5cm from the desired length when measured from the neck, accounting for room to pee; the model for size 2 is a male dog).

Next row (RS): k1, p2, *k2, p2* to the end of the row.

Next row (WS): *k2, p2*, repeat *–* until 3 sts remain, k2, p1.

Repeat these two rows until you have 5cm of ribbing. Cast (bind) off the sts.

Sleeves

Using 3.5mm (US 4) needles cast on 33 (28, 48) sts in the MC.

Size 1 only:

Row 1 (RS): k1, repeat *p2, k2* to the end of the row.

Row 2 (WS): *p2, k2*, repeat *–* until 1 st remains, p1.

Sizes 2 and 3 only:

Row 1 (RS): Repeat *k2, p2* until the end of the row.

Row 2 (WS): Repeat *k2, p2* until the end of the row.

All sizes:

Repeat rows 1 and 2 until you have 5cm of ribbing. Swap to 4mm (US 6) needles. The sts are worked in stocking stitch. Begin the increases immediately in the first row.

Increase row (RS): k1, M1R, knit until 1 st remains, M1L, k1. *[2 sts increased]*

Repeat the increase row every 5th (12th, 12th) row another 5 (5, 8) times.

Note: On the WS, knit the increases M1R and M1L purlwise.

You should now have 45 (40, 66) sts. Knit another 2 (2, 3) rows in stocking stitch.

Cast off the sts and repeat for the second sleeve.

Finishing

Sew the front seam of the back panel closed along the length of the top ribbing. Sew the triangle on the upper part of the belly panel to the sides of the back panel for 10 (14, 36)cm (check the height on your dog). Leave a 10 (9, 15)cm gap between the panels for the sleeves and continue sewing the side seams up to the bottom edge of the ribbing on the belly panel.

In the MC and using 3.5mm (US 4) needles, pick up and knit 103 (111, 189) sts from the lower curve of the back panel.

Sizes 1 and 2 only:

Row 1 (RS): k1, p2, repeat *k2, p2* to the end of the row.

Size 3 only:

Row 1 (RS): k1, repeat *p2, k2* to the end of the row.

All sizes:

Row 2 (WS): Cast (bind) off 4 sts, knit ribbing to the end of the row.

Row 3 (RS): Cast (bind) off 4 sts, knit ribbing to the end of the row.

Repeat rows 2 and 3 until you have 5cm of ribbing.

Cast off the remaining sts.

Sew the sleeve side seams. Sew the sleeves into the sleeve holes so that their vertical seams are to the back of the side seams. Sew in the ends.

Put the sweater on your reluctant pet. Take a deep breath and go for a well-deserved afternoon walk to hear compliments on your matching sweaters.

The sweater for dogs is knitted in sections from the top down. The underbelly panel is knitted separately so that the sweater is easier to adjust for dogs of different chest sizes.

TIP

˅ ˅ ˅ ˅ ˅

You can easily adjust the room to pee under the belly depending on your pet's 'handiwork'. (The designer's ten-year-old furry friend can skilfully write his initial 'M' in cursive much better than many schoolchildren can nowadays – in pale yellow ink on white snow, of course).

Chart for the dog version of the sweater (Note that the chart is in two parts)

MC
CC1
CC2
CC3

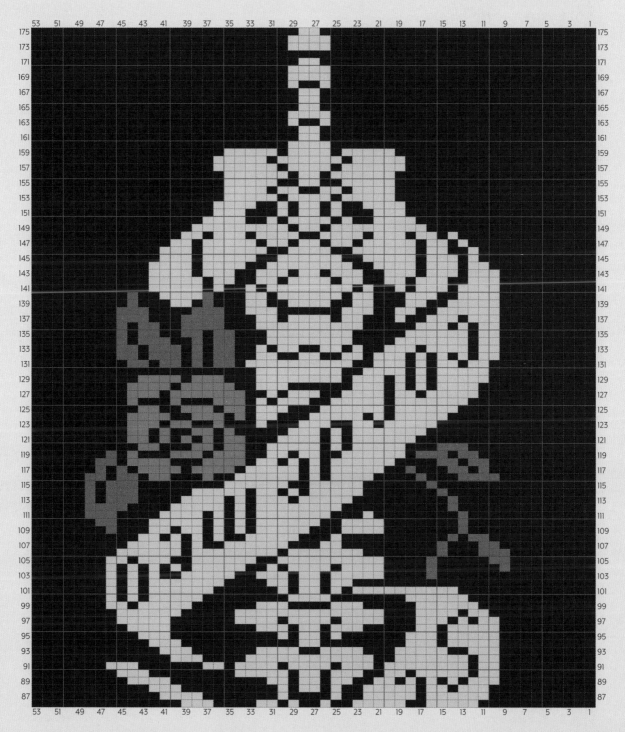

Blank ribbon chart for the human version of the sweater

MC

Lettering charts for the human version of the sweater

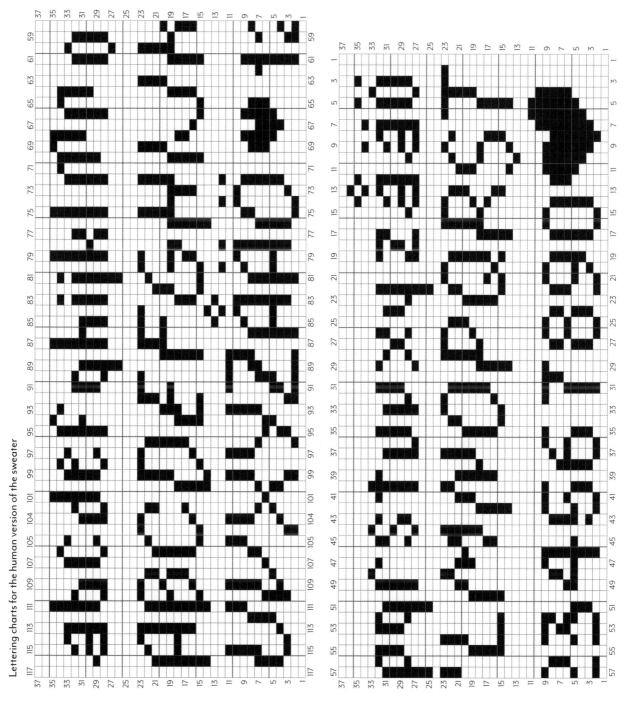

Blank ribbon chart for the dog version of the sweater

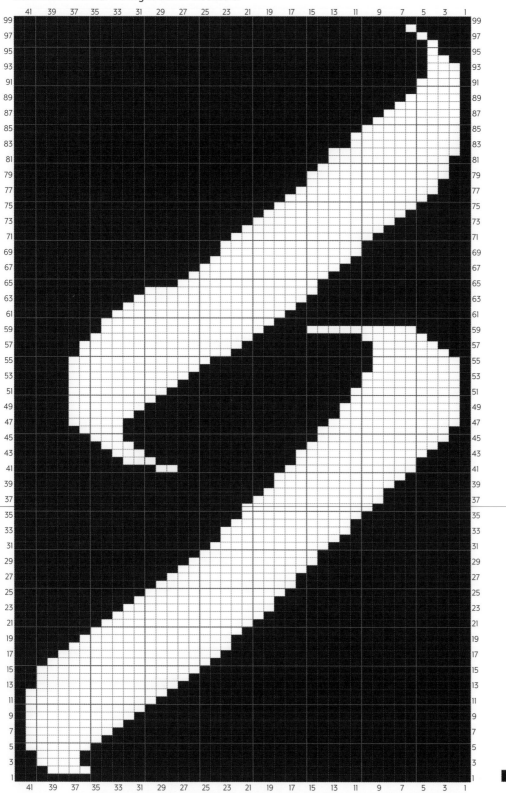

■ MC

Lettering charts for the dog version of the sweater

German Spitzes (Mittels) don't really need clothes, as they have a weather-resistant double coat, but this isn't the case for their owners. The 'smiling' Mittelspitz in this knit is my late dog Tico, whose face I captured in a knitting pattern years ago. He was my first Mittelspitz and left pawprints on my heart when he crossed the rainbow bridge at Christmas in 2019.

Mitteli

∨ ∨ ∨ ∨ ∨

MERJA OJANPERÄ

www.merjadesign.com
FB Merja Ojanperä Designs
IG @merjaojanpera

for humans

Shown in size S

Sizes: XS (S, M, L) (XL, XXL, 3XL, 4XL)

Recommended ease 2–4cm

Measurements of finished sweater

Chest circumference: 78 (89, 100, 111) (122, 133.5, 144.5, 155.5)cm

Length from armpit to hem: 37 (38, 39, 40) (41, 43, 45, 46)cm

Front length, neck to hem: 56 (59.5, 63, 67) (70.5, 73.5, 78, 82)cm

Upper sleeve circumference: 31 (33.5, 34.5, 35.5) (38, 39, 41, 43.5)cm

Wrist circumference: 22 (22, 23.5, 23.5) (24.5, 25.5, 25.5, 26.5)cm

Underarm sleeve length: 37 (38, 39, 41) (43, 45, 48, 50)cm

Yarn

Novita 7 Veljestä Nummi (76% wool, 20% polyamide, 4% viscose; 200m/100g) or equivalent worsted/Aran weight yarn

MC: 945 Frost 4 (5, 5, 5) (5, 5, 6, 7) skeins or 800 (1000, 1000, 1000) (1000, 1000, 1200, 1400)m

Novita Wool Rescue (75% recycled wool, 25% polyamide; 200m/100g) or equivalent worsted/Aran weight yarn

CC1: 289 Honey 1 (1, 1, 1) (1, 1, 2, 2) skein(s) or 200 (200, 200, 200) (200, 200, 400, 400)m

Novita 7 Veljestä (75% wool, 25% polyamide; 200m/100g) or equivalent worsted/Aran weight yarn

CC2: 064 False morel 1 (1, 1, 1) (1, 1, 2, 2) skein(s) or 200 (200, 200, 200) (200, 200, 400, 400)m

CC3: a little 525 Geisha for Swiss darning

Notions and tension (gauge)

Needles: 80–100cm circular needles and either double-pointed or 40cm circular needles for the sleeves, in sizes 4mm (US 6) and 4.5mm (US 7)

You will also need: Stitch markers, stitch holders or spare yarn, tapestry needle

Tension: 18 sts and 24 rows = 10 x 10cm in stocking (stockinette) stitch on 4.5mm (US 7) needles, blocked

for dogs

Model: Mittelspitz (size 2)

Sizes: 1 (2, 3)

Neck circumference: 39 (50, 61)cm

Chest circumference: 44.5 (55.5, 66.5)cm

Waist circumference: 38 (46.5, 55.5)cm

Back length: 30 (36.5, 46)cm

Yarn

Novita 7 Veljestä Nummi (76% wool, 20% polyamide, 4% viscose; 200m/100g) or equivalent worsted/Aran weight yarn

MC: 945 Frost 1 (1, 2) skein(s) or 200 (200, 400)m

Novita Wool Rescue (75% recycled wool, 25% polyamide; 200m/100g) or equivalent worsted/Aran weight yarn

CC1: 289 Honey 1 (1, 1) skein or 200 (200, 200, 200)m

Novita 7 Veljestä (75% wool, 25% polyamide; 200m/100g) or equivalent worsted/Aran weight yarn

CC2: 064 False morel 1 (1, 1) skein or 200 (200, 200, 200)m

Notions and tension (gauge)

Needles: 80–100cm circular needles and either double-pointed needles or 40cm circular needles for the sleeves, in sizes 4mm (US 6) and 4.5mm (US 7)

You will also need: Stitch markers, stitch holders or spare yarn, tapestry needle

Tension: 18 sts and 24 rows = 10 x 10cm in stocking stitch on 4.5mm (US 7) needles, blocked

The body and sleeves are knitted in the round from the bottom up and joined at the armpits. The sweater has a raglan yoke and a raised back neck for an improved fit. The pattern is completed with Swiss darning.

ⱽ ⱽ ⱽ ⱽ ⱽ

Don't forget to check the tension (gauge) for colourwork and use a larger needle size if necessary.

Mitteli for humans

Body

On 4mm (US 6) circular needles cast on 140 (160, 180, 200) (220, 240, 260, 280) sts in CC1. Join in the round, PM to mark the start of the round (left side). Add another stitch marker after 70 (80, 90, 100) (110, 120, 130, 140) sts (right side).

Knit *k1tbl, p1* ribbing for 8 (10, 10, 10) (12, 12, 14, 16) rounds. Swap to 4.5mm (US 7) needles and begin the colourwork following chart A. The pattern repeats 7 (8, 9, 10) (11, 12, 13, 14) times per round. Knit all 35 rows of the chart, cut the CCs.

Continue in stocking (stockinette) stitch in the MC until the length of the work measures 37 (38, 39, 40) (41, 43, 45, 46)cm from the hem to the armpit, or the hem is the desired length.

Next round: Knit until 4 (4, 4, 4) (5, 5, 6, 7) sts remain. Put the next 8 (8, 8, 8) (10, 10, 12, 14) sts onto a stitch holder (removing the marker). The yarn from the work is left at the border between the back panel and left sleeve. Set the body aside and knit the sleeves next.

Sleeves

Using 4mm (US 6) needles, cast on 40 (40, 42, 42) (44, 46, 46, 48) sts in the MC. Join in the round, PM. Work *k1tbl, p1* ribbing for 8 (10, 10, 10) (12, 12, 14, 16) rounds.

Swap to 4.5mm (US 7) needles. Knit 1 round, evenly increasing 8 (8, 6, 6) (4, 10, 10, 8) sts. You should now have 48 (48, 48, 48) (48, 56, 56, 56) sts.

Begin the colourwork following chart B; the pattern repeats 6 (6, 6, 6) (6, 7, 7, 7) times per round. Knit all 6 rows of the chart and then cut CV2.

Continue in stocking stitch in the MC and begin increases immediately after the chart.

Increase round: k1, M1L, knit until 1 st remains, M1R, k1.

[2 sts increased]

Repeat the increase row every 7th (7th, 7th, 7th) (8th, 8th, 9th, 9th) round another 3 (5, 6, 7) (9, 6, 8, 10) times. You should now have 56 (60, 62, 64) (68, 70, 74, 78) sts.

Continue in stocking stitch until the length of the sleeve is 37 (38, 39, 41) (43, 45, 48, 50)cm.

Next round: Knit until 4 (4, 4, 4) (5, 5, 6, 7) sts remain. Put the next 8 (8, 8, 8) (10, 10, 12, 14) sts onto a stitch holder (removing the marker).

Repeat for the other sleeve.

Yoke

Join the body and sleeves. Continue in the MC using 4.5mm (US 7) needles. Knit the 48 (52, 54, 56) (58, 60, 62, 64) sts for the left sleeve, PM (centre of 1st raglan seam), knit the 62 (72, 82, 92) (100, 110, 118, 126) sts for the front, place the next 8 (8, 8, 8) (10, 10, 12, 14) sts onto a stitch holder (removing the marker), PM, knit the 48 (52, 54, 56) (58, 60, 62, 64) sts for the right sleeve, PM, knit the 62 (72, 82, 92) (100, 110, 118, 126) sts for the back, PM (this is the round marker). The start of the round is now the seam between the back section and left sleeve. You should now have 220 (248, 272, 296) (316, 340, 360, 380 sts. Knit another 3 (3, 3, 4) (4, 4, 4, 5) rounds in stocking stitch in the MC.

Begin the raglan decreases:

Round 1 (decrease): k1, k2tog, knit until 3 sts remain before the marker, ssk, k1, SM*, repeat *–* 3 more times. *[8 sts decreased]*

Round 2: Knit until the end of the round.

Repeat rounds 1 and 2 another 16 (19, 22, 24) (25, 26, 27, 29) times. You should now have 84 (88, 88, 96) (108, 124, 136, 148) sts.

The length of the raglan seam is approx. 14 (16.5, 19, 21) (21.5, 22.5, 23.5, 24)cm before the neck raise.

Raise the back of the neck using short rows. If the neck feels large, you can continue the same raglan decreases on the RS of the front and back of the work for as long as you need.

Short rows:

Row 1 (RS): Knit to marker, SM, k4, turn.

Row 2 (WS): DS, *purl to marker, SM* 4 times, p4, turn.

Row 3 (RS): DS, *knit to row marker, SM* 4 times, knit to DS, knit the DS as a single st, k2, turn.

Row 4 (WS): DS, *purl to row marker, SM* 4 times, purl to DS, work the DS as a single st, p2, turn work.

Row 5 (RS): DS, *knit to marker, SM* twice, knit to round marker.

Finally, knit 1 round (knit DSs as single sts), evenly decreasing 4 (6, 4, 10) (20, 30, 38, 48) sts. You should now have 80 (82, 84, 86) (88, 94, 98, 100) sts.

Swap to 4mm (US 6) needles and knit *k1tbl, p1* ribbing for 6 (7, 7, 7) (8, 8, 8, 8) rounds, or until the desired length.

Cast (bind) off using a stretchy cast-off method.

Finishing

Join the armpits using kitchener stitch and weave in all the ends on the WS of the work. Wet the sweater, lay it out and shape it to its final measurements. Leave to dry flat.

Chart A

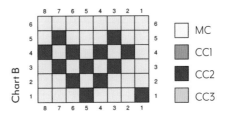

Chart B

□ MC

▨ CC1

■ CC2

▨ CC3

Mitteli for dogs

Using 4mm (US 6) double-pointed needles or a circular needle, cast on 70 (90, 110) sts in CC1 using your preferred stretchy cast-on method. The start of a new round will be at the centre of the belly.

Work *k1tbl, p1* ribbing for 8 (10, 12)cm or your desired length for the collar.

Swap to 4.5mm (US 7) double-pointed or circular needles. Knit 2 rounds, evenly increasing 10 sts in every size. You should now have 80 (100, 120) sts. Now knit all the rows of the chart; the pattern repeats 4 (5, 6) times per round. Then continue to knit in the MC.

Once the work measures 8 (10, 12)cm from the bottom of the ribbing, divide the work as follows for the sleeves:

Next round: RM, k10 (12, 14), cast (bind) off 1 st, knit until 11 (13, 15) sts remain on the round and cast off 1 st. Now knit the next 20 (24, 28) sts onto double-pointed needles for the front and place the remaining sts (for the back) on a stitch holder or spare yarn. Turn.

Next row (WS): Purl to the end of the row.

Next row (RS): Knit to the end of the row.

Repeat these two rows until the work measures 8 (9, 10)cm from the division or the preferred length for your dog. End on a WS row. Set the sts aside.

Go back to the 58 (74, 90) sts for the back, and work in stocking (stockinette) stitch until the back measures the same as the centre panel. End on a purl row.

Join in the round again as follows:

PM (this is the new round marker), knit the back sts, PM, cast on 1 st, PM, knit the centre sts, PM, cast on 1 st. You should now have 80 (100, 120) sts again.

Knit 5 (6, 7) rounds and then knit decreases.

Decrease round: SM, k2tog, knit until 2 sts remain before the marker, k2tog tbl, SM, k1, SM, k2tog, knit until 2 sts remain before the marker, k2tog tbl, SM, k1, SM. *[4 sts decreased]*

Repeat the decrease round another 2 (3, 4) times. You can leave these decreases out if a straighter design would suit your dog better, or even increase the number of decreases as necessary.

Once the work measures 20 (25, 32)cm in length, or is a suitable length for your dog, place the sts for the belly between the markers onto a stitch holder and continue knitting the 52 (66, 80) sts flat.

Row 1 (RS): Cast off 2 sts, knit to the end of the row.

Row 2 (WS): Cast off 2 sts, purl to the end of the row.

Repeat rows 1–2 another 3 (4, 5) times.

Next row (RS): Cast off 1 st, knit to the end of the row.

Next row (WS): Cast off 1 st, purl to the end of the row.

Repeat these 2 rows 3 (4, 5) more times. You should now have 28 (36, 44) sts.

Mitteli for dogs is knitted from the neck to the hem in the round using double-pointed or circular needles. To finish, stitches are picked up from the hem and front leg holes and are worked in ribbing.

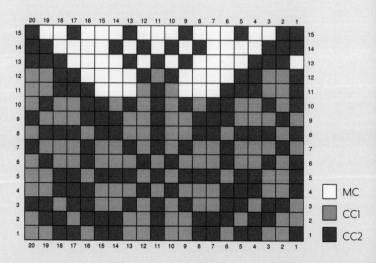

Finishing

In the MC, pick up and knit sts from the hem in addition to the sts on your needles so that you have a total of 72 (90, 108) sts. Swap to 4mm (US 6) needles and work 8 (8, 10) rows of *k1tbl, p1* ribbing. Cast off in ribbing using a stretchy cast off method.

In the MC and using double-pointed needles, pick up and knit 44 (50, 56) sts from the edges of the sleeve hole.

Work *k1tbl, p1* ribbing for 8 (10, 12) rows or until you reach the desired length. Cast off loosely in ribbing. Repeat for the other sleeve.

Weave in the ends on the wrong side of the work. Wet the sweater, lay it out and adjust it to its final measurements. Leave to dry flat.

TIP

ᐯ ᐯ ᐯ ᐯ ᐯ

Please note that the distance between the front legs varies from dog to dog. For small dogs, the distance is often relatively larger than in larger dogs. For this reason, measure the distance between the front legs from under the belly and check that the sleeve holes are a suitable distance apart. The back can be knitted shorter or longer, and the decreases after the sleeve holes can be left out, if necessary.

The Mittelspitz is a happy and energetic dog that enjoys a range of hobbies and activities. Other German Spitz breeds are the Pomeranian (Zwergspitz), the Kleinspitz, the Keeshond (Wolfspitz) and the Giant Spitz (Großspitz). Perhaps the most visible difference between these similar breeds is their size, which is how they are classified. It isn't unusual for a Kleinspitz to be reclassified as a Mittelspitz after an official measurement. Personally, I've only owned Kleinspitzes and Mittelspitzes, but it's my dream to own a Keeshond one day.

As every dog owner knows, dogs are man's best friend. They show their unconditional love come rain or shine, and they are fantastic companions for hiking and all kinds of activities. You can cry or whisper your deepest secrets into a dog's fur, and they will always comfort you and cheer you up.

I designed the Sydänystävä set for the lovely Viva and gorgeous long-haired Dachshund, Didi. The set can easily be adjusted for dogs of different sizes, and the Dachshund pattern on the hem can be replaced with the pawprints in the pattern if you'd like to make the sweater for another breed of dog.

Sydänystävä

∨ ∨ ∨ ∨ ∨

PIRJO
IIVONEN
IG unelmiensilmukat
FB unelmiensilmukat

for humans

Shown in size M
Sizes: S (M, L, XL)
Recommended ease 5–10cm

vvvvvvvvvvvvvvvvvvvvvvvvvvvvvvvvvvvv

Measurements of finished sweater
Chest circumference: 84 (94.5, 105.5, 116)cm
Length from armpit to hem: 43 (44, 45, 46)cm
Front length, neck to hem: 67.5 (68.5, 70.5, 73)cm
Upper sleeve circumference: 37 (38, 39, 40)cm
Wrist circumference: 23 (23, 24, 24)cm
Underarm sleeve length: 44 (45, 45, 46)cm

vvvvvvvvvvvvvvvvvvvvvvvvvvvvvvvvvvvv

Yarn
Cascade Yarns 220 (100% wool; 200m/100g) or equivalent DK weight yarn
MC: 2442 Fog hatt 3 (3, 4, 4) hanks or 550 (600, 700, 800)m
CC1: 9684 Green tea 1 (1, 1, 2) hank(s) or 100 (150, 200, 300)m
CC2: 8686 Brown 1 (1, 1, 2) hank(s) or 100 (150, 200, 300)m
CC3: 2414 Ginger 1 (1, 1, 2) hank(s) or 100 (150, 200, 300)m
CC4: 2415 Sunflower 1 (1, 1, 1) hank or 100 (150, 150, 200)m

vvvvvvvvvvvvvvvvvvvvvvvvvvvvvvvvvvvv

Notions and gauge
Needles: 80–100cm circular needles and, if necessary, double-pointed needles, in sizes 4mm (US 6) and 4.5mm (US 7)
You will also need: Stitch markers, stitch holders or spare yarn, tapestry needle
Tension: 19 sts and 26 rows = 10 x 10cm in stocking (stockinette) stitch on 4mm (US 6) needles, lightly blocked. Knit a swatch in colourwork and adjust your needle size if necessary.

for dogs

Model: Long-haired Dachshund (size 1)
Sizes: 1 (2, 3)
Recommended ease 2–5cm for ease of movement

Measurements of finished sweater
Neck circumference: 28.5 (31.5, 34.5)cm
Chest circumference: 46.5 (50.5, 63)cm
Waist circumference: 34.5 (37, 44)cm
Back length: adjustable
Sleeve length: adjustable
Distance between front legs at armpits: 7.5 (7.5, 9.5)cm

Yarn
Cascade Yarns 220 (100% wool; 200m/100g) or equivalent DK weight yarn
MC: 2442 Fog hatt 1 (2, 2) hank(s) or 200 (300, 400)m
CC1: 9684 Green tea 1 (1, 1) hank or 80 (110, 150)m
CC2: 8686 Brown 1 (1, 1) hank or 50 (80, 120)m
CC3: 2414 Ginger 1 (1, 1) hank or 50 (80, 120)m
CC4: 2415 Sunflower 1 (1, 1) hank or 80 (100, 150)m

Notions and gauge
Needles: 80–100cm circular needles and double-pointed needles in sizes 4mm (US 6) and 4.5mm (US 7)
You will also need: Stitch markers, spare yarn, tapestry needle
Tension: 19 sts and 26 rows = 10 x 10cm in stocking stitch on 4mm (US 6) needles, lightly blocked. Knit a swatch in colourwork and adjust your needle size if necessary.

ⱽ ⱽ ⱽ ⱽ ⱽ

In colourwork sections, if you are carrying yarn across the WS for more then 4 sts, trap the floats at the back of the work to avoid them becoming too long.

Sydänystävä for humans

Body

Using 4mm (US 6) needles and CC1, cast on 160
(180, 200, 220) sts. Join in the round, being careful to
avoid twisting the work. PM at the start of the round
(centre back).

Work 4cm of *k1, p1* ribbing and then one round in
stocking (stockinette) stitch.

Swap to 4.5mm (US 7) needles and knit chart A, working
in all the colours. If you wish, you can place a stitch
marker every 20 sts to make it easier to follow the chart.
The pattern repeats 8 (9, 10, 11) times in a round. Once
you've knitted all 36 rows of chart A, cut the CCs and
remove all stitch markers except for the round marker.
For sizes S and L, move the start of the round by knitting
10 sts and placing the marker so that the centre front
marked on the chart is at the centre of the front panel (in
sizes M and XL, the start of the round stays where it is).
Continue in stocking stitch in the MC on 4mm (US 6)
needles until the body section measures 43 (44, 45,
46)cm from the cast-on edge and you are at the start of
the round. Set the body aside and knit the sleeves next.

Sleeves

Using 4mm (US 6) needles and CC1, cast on 44 (44, 46,
46) sts. Join in the round, being careful not to twist, PM
at the start of the round (on the side seam of the sleeve,
under the armpit). Work *k1, p1* ribbing for 5cm. Then
work one round, evenly increasing 16 (16, 14, 14) sts.
You should now have 60 (60, 60, 60) sts. Work two
more rounds.

Swap to 4.5mm (US 7) needles and knit chart B, working
in all the colours. The pattern repeats 12 (12, 12, 12)
times in a round. Once you have knitted all 14 rows of
chart B, cut the CCs. Continue in stocking stitch in the
MC on 4mm (US 6) needles. Knit 1 round and then knit
the increases.

Increase round: k1, M1L, knit until 1 st remains, M1R, k1.
[2 sts increased]

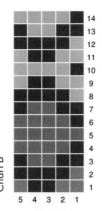

Chart B

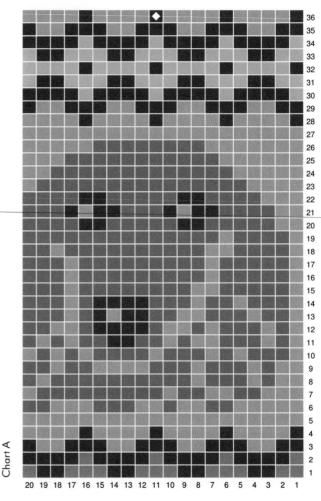

Chart A

Repeat the increase round every 4cm another 4 (5, 6, 7) times. You should now have 70 (72, 74, 76) sts.

Continue knitting in stocking stitch until the length of the sleeve from the cast-on edge is 44 (45, 45, 46)cm.

Place 5 (7, 8, 10) sts from the start of the round and 5 (7, 8, 10) sts from the end of the round onto a stitch holder or spare yarn, totalling 10 (14, 16, 20) armpit sts.

Repeat for the other sleeve.

Yoke

Now combine the body and the sleeves. Continue knitting in the MC with 4mm (US 6) needles. Knit 35 (38, 42, 45) sts of the body, PM, place the next 10 (14, 16, 20) sts onto a stitch holder or spare yarn, join the first sleeve by knitting the 60 (58, 58, 56) sts onto the circular needles, PM. Knit 70 (76, 84, 90) sts, PM, place the next 10 (14, 16, 20) sts onto spare yarn, join the second sleeve by knitting the 60 (58, 58, 56) sleeve sts, PM. Knit the final 35 (38, 42, 45) sts of the round. You should now have 260 (268, 284, 292) sts.

Next round:

Size S: Knit until the end of the round.

Size M: Knit until 1 st remains on the right sleeve, knit the strand between the sts in the previous row tbl, knit until 1 st remains before the left sleeve, knit the strand between the sts in the previous row tbl, knit to the end of the round. *[2 sts increased]*

Size L: Knit until 1 st remains before the right sleeve, k2tog, knit until 1 sleeve st remains, k2tog, knit until 1 st remains before the left sleeve, k2tog, knit until 1 sleeve st remains, k2tog, knit to the end of the round. *[4 sts decreased]*

Size XL: Knit until 1 st remains on the right sleeve, k2tog, knit until 1 st remains on the left sleeve, k2tog, knit to the end of the round. *[2 sts decreased]*

You should now have 260 (270, 280, 290) sts.

Knit 0 (0, 3, 6) rounds.

Continue knitting chart C on 4.5mm (US 7) needles. The pattern repeats 26 (27, 28, 29) times in a round. Knit all 52 rows of the chart. You should now have 104 (108, 112, 116) sts.

Cut the CCs and continue in the MC on 4mm (US 6) needles.

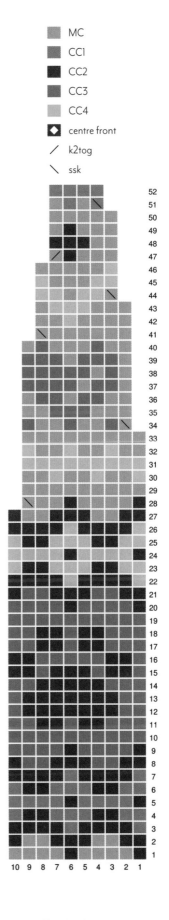

Chart C

MC
CC1
CC2
CC3
CC4
◇ centre front
／ k2tog
＼ ssk

Neck

Remove all stitch markers except for the one at the start of the round.

If you like, you can raise the back slightly using short rows as follows:

Row 1 (RS): Knit 10 (10, 10, 10), turn.

Row 2 (WS): DS, purl to round marker, SM, p10 (10, 10, 10), turn.

Row 3: DS, knit to round marker, SM, knit to DS, work the DS as a single st, k10 (10, 10, 10), turn.

Row 4: DS, purl to round marker, SM, purl to DS, work the DS as a single st, p10 (10, 10, 10), turn.

Row 5: DS, knit to round marker, SM, knit to DS, work the DS as a single st, k10 (10, 10, 10), turn.

Row 6: DS, purl to round marker, SM, purl to DS, work the DS as a single st, p10 (10, 10, 10), turn.

Row 7: DS, knit to round marker, SM, knit to DS, work the DS as a single st, k10 (10, 10, 10), turn.

Row 8: DS, purl to round marker, SM, purl to DS, work the DS as a single st, p10 (10, 10, 10), turn.

Row 9: DS, knit to round marker, SM, knit to the end of the round (work the DSs on the row as single sts).

Knit 1 more round and evenly decrease 14 (16, 18, 20) sts. Work *k1, p1* ribbing for another 3cm or until the neck is the desired length.

Cast (bind) off in ribbing using a stretchy cast off method.

Finishing

Kitchener stitch the armpits closed and sew in the ends. Wash the sweater in lukewarm water, squeeze inside a terry towel to remove excess water, shape on a flat surface, and leave to dry flat.

Sydänystävä **for dogs**

Body

Knit the neck in ribbing.

Note: When knitting, choose a place to put a hole so you can attach a lead to the collar or harness: for a collar, place a buttonhole in the middle of the back of the neck immediately after the neck ribbing; for a harness, place the hole after the colourwork in stocking (stockinette) stitch wherever you will attach the lead to the harness.

Make the buttonhole as follows: at the desired spot, k2tog, yo, and on the next round, knit the decreased stitch then knit the yo tbl. This will create a small hole.

Using 4mm (US 6) needles and CC1, cast on 54 (60, 66) sts. Join in the round, being careful to avoid twisting the work. PM at the start of the round (centre front). Work *k1, p1* ribbing for 4 (6, 8)cm and then work 1 round, evenly increasing 1 (0, 9) sts.

Swap to the 4.5mm (US 7) needles while you knit the colourwork. Working in all the colours, knit the chart; the pattern will repeat 11 (12, 15) times per round. If your dog has a deep chest or a larger chest circumference than allowed for in the pattern measurements, you can add the required number of sts on row 19 of the chart – note that the number of sts you add must be divisible by 4. Knit all 28 rows of the chart and then cut the CCs and continue in the MC on 4mm (US 6) needles. Once you have finished the chart, try the sweater on your dog and add sts as needed to make sure that it isn't tight around their chest. Once the work is long enough from the neck for the front edge to reach the front legs, use spare yarn to make places for the sleeves as follows:

Knit 7 (7, 9) sts, then take a piece of spare yarn and knit the following 18 (18, 22) sts onto it, place the sts knitted onto the spare yarn back onto the left needle and then knit them again in the MC. Knit in the MC until 25 (25, 31) sts remain in the round, take another piece of spare yarn and then knit the next 18 (18, 22) sts onto it, move

the sts knitted onto the spare yarn back onto the left
needle, and then knit them again in the MC. You have
now made places for the sleeves as you would make
thumbholes in gloves.

Continue to knit in stocking stitch, decreasing every 4th
round as follows: k1, ssk, knit until 3 sts remain, k2tog. k1.
Repeat these decreases another 10 (12, 17) times, or until
you reach the desired length for a male dog.

Now knit flat.

Next row (RS): Cast off 6 (8, 12) sts, knit to the end of
the row.

Next row (WS): Cast off 6 (8, 12) sts, purl to the end of
the row.

Next row (RS): k1, ssk, knit until 3 sts remain, k2tog, k1.

Next row (WS): Purl to the end of the row.

Repeat the last 2 rows until the work is the same length
as the dog's back measured from the bottom edge of the
neck. Pick up an even number of sts from the end of the
work for border ribbing. Work *k1, p1* ribbing for
2cm and then cast off using a stretchy cast-off method.

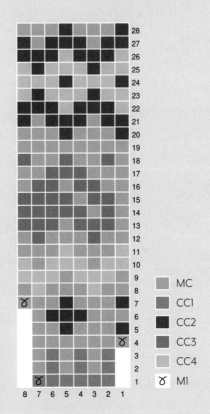

- MC
- CC1
- CC2
- CC3
- CC4
- ✗ M1

TIP

The pattern has three sizes to fit small dogs (1),
small-to-medium dogs, such as a Shetland sheep-
dog (2) and medium dogs, such as a collie (3).
As the sweater is worked as a single piece from the
top down, and the colour pattern is on the yoke,
you'll find it easy to adjust the fit for your dog.

Sleeves

Pick up the sleeve sts from both sides of the spare yarn onto 4mm (US 6) needles. Remove the spare yarn. Pick up another 3 sts from both sides of the hole. The sleeve now has 42 (42, 50) sts. Work in stocking (stockinette) stitch in the MC until the sleeve is 6cm shorter than the dog's front leg. Evenly decrease 10 (10, 16) sts. Then work *k1, p1* ribbing for 3cm.

Cast (bind) off using a stretchy cast-off method.

Finishing

Sew all the ends into the wrong side of the work. Wash the sweater in lukewarm water, squeeze inside a terry towel to remove excess water, shape on a flat surface, and leave to dry flat.

TIP

ⴸ ⴸ ⴸ ⴸ ⴸ

For male dogs, knit flat once the edge of the belly panel is approx. 5cm from the penis to avoid getting droplets on the sweater.

Borg means 'city' in Icelandic, and this design is inspired by the countless walks I've been on with my husband and our Chihuahua in Reykjavik, Rome and New York. We are both big fans of Icelandic knitting, and our dog loves Icelandic wool. If any felt or a sweater I've knitted is left within reach, we're guaranteed to find our dog sleeping on top of it.

The Borg sweater works in a range of colour combinations, and you might like to design your colourways to match the feel of different seasons or weather. The lightness, breathability and practicality of a lopapeysa (Icelandic sweater) make it a great outer layer.

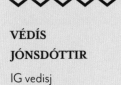

VÉDÍS
JÓNSDÓTTIR
IG vedisj

for humans

Shown in size XL
Sizes: S (M, L, XL, 2XL)

⌄⌄⌄⌄⌄⌄⌄⌄⌄⌄⌄⌄⌄⌄⌄⌄⌄⌄⌄⌄⌄⌄⌄⌄⌄⌄⌄⌄

Measurements of finished sweater
Chest circumference: 89 (98, 106.5, 115.5, 124.5)cm
Length from armpit to hem: 41 (42, 43, 44, 45)cm
Upper sleeve circumference: 38 (40, 42, 44.5, 46.5)cm
Wrist circumference: 22 (23.5, 24.5, 25.5, 26.5)cm
Underarm sleeve length: 58 (60, 62, 64, 66)cm

⌄⌄⌄⌄⌄⌄⌄⌄⌄⌄⌄⌄⌄⌄⌄⌄⌄⌄⌄⌄⌄⌄⌄⌄⌄⌄⌄⌄

Yarn

Istex Lettlopi (100% wool; 100m/50g) or equivalent Aran weight yarn

MC: 0005 Black heather 7 (8, 8, 9, 10) skeins or 700 (800, 800, 900, 1000)m
CC1: 0058 Dark grey heather 2 (2, 2, 2, 2) skeins or 200 (200, 200, 200, 200)m
CC2: 0054 Light ash heather 1 (1, 1, 2, 2) skeins or 100 (100, 100, 200, 200)m
CC3: 1704 Apricot 1 (1, 1, 1, 1) skeins or 100 (100, 100, 100, 100)m
CC4: 1703 Mimosa 1 (1, 1, 1, 1) skeins or 100 (100, 100, 100, 100)m
CC5: 1700 Air blue 1 (1, 1, 1, 1) skein or 100 (100, 100, 100, 100)m

⌄⌄⌄⌄⌄⌄⌄⌄⌄⌄⌄⌄⌄⌄⌄⌄⌄⌄⌄⌄⌄⌄⌄⌄⌄⌄⌄⌄

Notions and tension (gauge)

Needles: 40cm and 80cm circular needles plus double-pointed needles in sizes 3.5mm (US 4) and 4.5mm (US 7)
You will also need: Stitch markers, stitch holders or spare yarn, tapestry needle
Tension: 18 sts and 24 rows = 10 x 10cm in stocking (stockinette) stitch on 4.5mm (US 7) needles, lightly blocked. Knit a swatch in colourwork and adjust your needle size if necessary.

for dogs

Model: Chihuahua (size 2)
Sizes: 1 (2, 3, 4)

Measurements of finished sweater
Neck circumference: adjustable
Chest circumference: 44.5 (49, 53.5, 58)cm
Waist circumference: 31 (35.5, 40, 44.5)cm
Back length: 24.5 (29, 33.5, 39)cm

Yarn

Istex Lettlopi (100% wool; 100m/50g) or equivalent Aran weight yarn

MC: 0005 Black heather 1 (1, 2, 2) skein(s) or 100 (100, 200, 200)m
CC1: 0058 Dark grey heather 1 (1, 1, 1) skein or 100 (100, 100, 100)m
CC2: 0054 Light ash heather 1 (1, 1, 1) skein or 100 (100, 100, 100)m
CC3: 1704 Apricot 1 (1, 1, 1) skein or 100 (100, 100, 100)m
CC4: 1703 Mimosa 1 (1, 1, 1) skein or 100 (100, 100, 100)m
CC5: 1700 Air blue 1 (1, 1, 1) skein or 100 (100, 100, 100)m

Notions and tension (gauge)

Needles: 40cm and 80cm circular needles plus double-pointed needles in sizes 3.5mm (US 4) and 4.5mm (US 7)
You will also need: Stitch markers, stitch holders or spare yarn, tapestry needle
Tension: 18 sts and 24 rows = 10 x 10cm in stocking stitch on 4.5mm (US 7) needles, lightly blocked. Knit a swatch in colourwork and adjust your needle size if necessary.

Body

Using 3.5mm (US 4) circular needles, cast on 160 (176, 192, 208, 224) sts in the MC. Join in the round, PM to mark the start of the round (left side seam).

Work 3 rounds of *k1, p1* ribbing.

Work 2 rounds of ribbing in CC3. Swap to CC4 and work 2 rounds of ribbing.

Swap to the 4.5mm (US 7) circular needles and begin to knit chart A. The pattern repeats 40 (44, 48, 52, 56) times per round. Knit all 6 rows of the chart and then cut the CCs.

Continue in stocking stitch in the MC until work measures 41 (42, 43, 44, 45)cm.

Next round: k5 (6, 7, 8, 9) sts and place them onto a stitch holder, k80 (88, 96, 104, 112) sts, place the last 10 (12, 14, 16, 18) knitted sts onto another stitch holder, k70 (76, 82, 88, 94) sts, place the remaining 5 (6, 7, 8, 9) sts onto the same stitch holder that you used for the sts at the start of the round.

Sleeves

Using 3.5mm (US 4) double-pointed needles, cast on 40 (42, 44, 46, 48) sts in the MC. Join in the round, PM to mark the start of the round.

Work 3 rounds of *k1, p1* ribbing.

Work 2 rounds of ribbing in CC3. Swap to CC4 and work 2 rounds of ribbing. Evenly increase 4 (6, 4, 6, 4) sts on the last round. You will now have 44 (48, 48, 52, 52) sts.

Swap to the 4.5mm (US 7) double-pointed needles and begin to knit chart A. The pattern repeats 11 (12, 12, 13, 13) times per round. Knit all 6 rows of the chart and then cut the CCs. Continue in stocking stitch in the MC.

Knit 1 round and then begin to increase.

Increase round: K1, M1R, knit until 1 st remains, M1L, k1.

Repeat the increase round another 11 (11, 13, 13, 15) times every 7th (7th, 6th, 6th, 6th) round. You will now have 68 (72, 76, 80, 84) sts.

Continue in stocking stitch until the length of the sleeve is 49 (50, 51, 52, 53)cm.

Place 5 (6, 7, 8, 9) sts from both sides of the stitch marker onto a stitch holder or spare yarn, a total of 10 (12, 14, 16, 18) armpit sts.

Set the 58 (60, 62, 64, 66) sleeve sts aside and repeat for the other sleeve.

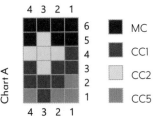

Chart A

4 3 2 1		
	6	■ MC
	5	
	4	■ CC1
	3	☐ CC2
	2	
	1	■ CC5

4 3 2 1

The sweater is knitted in the round from the bottom up.

Yoke

Join the sleeves and body as follows:

In the MC and using 4.5mm (US 7) circular needles, knit 29 (30, 31, 32, 33) sleeve sts, PM, knit the remaining 29 (30, 31, 32, 33) sleeve sts, knit the 70 (76, 82, 88, 94) sts for the front panel, knit 29 (30, 31, 32, 33) sleeve sts, PM, knit the remaining 29 (30, 31, 32, 33) sleeve sts, knit the 70 (76, 82, 88, 94) sts for the back panel, PM. The start of the round is now between the left sleeve and the back panel. You should now have 256 (272, 288, 304, 320) sts.

Begin chart B. The pattern repeats 8 (8.5, 9, 9.5, 10) times per round. Work the entire chart for size 2XL, but note that for the other sizes, you should skip certain rows as indicated on the chart.

Note for sizes M and XL: The final repeat of the pattern is half a repeat, so only knit sts 1–16!

Work the chart, decreasing according to the chart. Swap to shorter circular needles if necessary. You should now have 96 (102, 108, 114, 120) sts.

Short rows to raise the back neck:

Row 1 (RS): Knit until 6 sts remain before the marker, w&t.

Row 2 (WS): Purl to round marker, SM, purl until 6 sts remain before the marker, w&t.

Row 3: Knit to round marker, SM, knit until 3 sts remain before the marker (when you come to the wrapped st from the previous row, knit it together with its wrap), w&t.

Row 4: Purl to round marker, SM, purl until 3 sts remain before the marker (when you come to the wrapped st from the previous row, knit it together with its wrap), w&t.

Row 5: Knit to round marker, SM, knit to marker (when you come to the wrapped st from the previous row, knit it together with its wrap), w&t.

Row 6: Purl to round marker, SM, purl to marker (when you come to the wrapped st from the previous row, knit it together with its wrap), w&t.

Row 7: Knit to round marker, SM.

Neck

Swap to 3.5mm (US 4) needles and continue in the MC.

Knit 1 round, evenly decreasing 24 (28, 32, 36, 40) sts. You will now have 72 (74, 76, 78, 80) sts.

Knit 14 rounds of *k1, p1* ribbing.

Cast (bind) off using a stretchy cast-off method.

Finishing

Close the armpits using kitchener stitch. Fold the neck over to the WS and sew closed. Sew in the ends.

Wet the sweater in lukewarm water, shape it, and leave it to dry flat.

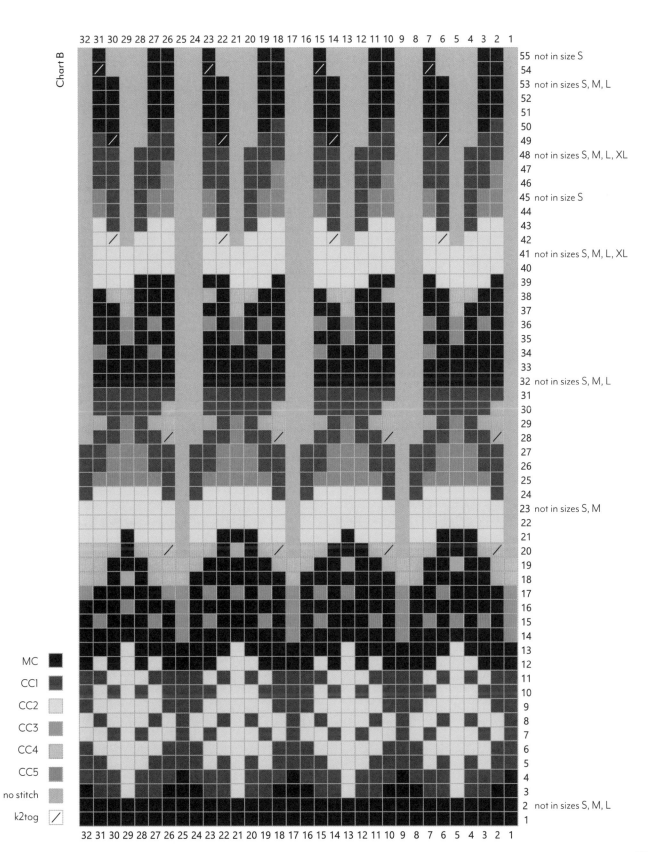

Chart B

| | 32 | 31 | 30 | 29 | 28 | 27 | 26 | 25 | 24 | 23 | 22 | 21 | 20 | 19 | 18 | 17 | 16 | 15 | 14 | 13 | 12 | 11 | 10 | 9 | 8 | 7 | 6 | 5 | 4 | 3 | 2 | 1 | |

55 not in size S
54
53 not in sizes S, M, L
52
51
50
49
48 not in sizes S, M, L, XL
47
46
45 not in size S
44
43
42
41 not in sizes S, M, L, XL
40
39
38
37
36
35
34
33
32 not in sizes S, M, L
31
30
29
28
27
26
25
24
23 not in sizes S, M
22
21
20
19
18
17
16
15
14
13
12
11
10
9
8
7
6
5
4
3
2 not in sizes S, M, L
1

MC ■
CC1 ■
CC2 □
CC3 ■
CC4 ■
CC5 ■
no stitch ■
k2tog ╱

32 31 30 29 28 27 26 25 24 23 22 21 20 19 18 17 16 15 14 13 12 11 10 9 8 7 6 5 4 3 2 1

Borg for dogs

Body

Using 4.5mm (US 7) circular needles, cast on 29 (33, 37, 41) sts in the MC. Work ribbing in rows as follows:

Row 1 (WS): k1, repeat *p1, k1* to the end of the row.

Row 2 (RS): p1, repeat *k1, p1* until the end of the row.

Repeat row 1 once more.

Next row (RS): p1, k1, p1, knit until 3 sts remain, p1, k1, p1.

Next row (WS): k1, p1, k1, purl until 3 sts remain, k1, p1, k1.

Repeat these two rows until the work measures 8 (10, 12, 14)cm. End on a wrong-side row.

Next row (RS): p1, k1, p1, knit until 3 sts remain, p1, k1, p1, PM (end of the back panel), cast on 27 (31, 35, 39) sts, PM (side marker). Join in the round, knit to the round marker. You should now have 56 (64, 72, 80) sts.

Next round (WS): k1, repeat *p1, k1* to the marker, SM, p1, k1. p1, knit until 3 sts remain before the marker, p1, k1, p1, SM.

Repeat the last round twice more.

Continue in stocking stitch until the work measures 16 (20, 24, 28)cm from the cast-on edge.

Set the work aside and knit the sleeves next.

Sleeves

Using 3.5mm (US 4) double-pointed needles, cast on 20 (22, 24, 24) sts in the MC. Join in the round, PM to mark the start of the round.

Work 3 rounds of *k1, p1* ribbing.

Swap to 4.5mm (US 7) double-pointed needles. Knit 1 round, evenly increasing 2 (2, 2, 2) sts. You should now have 22 (24, 26, 26) sts.

Continue in stocking stitch until the work measures 6 (7, 8, 9)cm. Transfer 2 (3, 3, 3) sts from the start of the round and 3 (3, 4, 4) sts from the end of the round to a stitch holder (underarm section). You should now have 17 (18, 19, 19) sts. Repeat for the other sleeve.

Yoke

Join the body and the sleeves in the MC using 4.5mm (US 7) needles.

Set-up round: k4 (4, 4, 5), place the next 5 (6, 7, 7) sts onto a stitch holder, knit the 17 (18, 19, 19) sleeve sts, knit the 9 (11, 13, 15) front sts, place the next 5 (6, 7, 7) sts onto a stitch holder, knit the 17 (18, 19, 19) sleeve sts, knit to marker, SM, knit to the end of the round.

You should now have 80 (88, 96, 104) sts.

Chart columns: 8 7 6 5 4 3 2 1

Rows:
25
24
23
22
21 not in sizes 1, 2, 3
20
19 not in sizes 1, 2, 3
18
17
16
15 not in sizes 1, 2
14 not in sizes 1, 2
13
12
11
10 not in sizes 1, 2, 3
9
8
7
6
5
4
3
2
1 not in size 1

Legend:
- ■ MC
- ■ CC1
- ☐ CC2
- ■ CC3
- ■ CC4
- ■ CC5
- ■ no stitch
- ⁄ k2tog

Short rows:

Short row 1 (RS): Knit to marker, SM, w&t. Turn.

Short row 2 (WS): SM, purl to marker, SM, w&t. Turn.

Begin to knit the chart; the pattern repeats 10 (11, 12, 13) times per round. Trap floats of more than 7 sts on the WS of the work. Work the entire chart for size 4, but note that for the other sizes you should skip certain rows as indicated on the chart.

Note: After row 9 of the chart, repeat short rows 1 and 2 one more time.

Knit all 19 (20, 22, 25) rows of the chart. You should now have 40 (44, 48, 52) sts.

Neck

Swap to CC3 and 3.5mm (US 4) needles.

Knit 1 round, evenly decreasing according to the circumference of the dog's head.

Work 1 round of *k1, p1* ribbing.

Swap to CC4 and work 2 rounds of ribbing.

Cast (bind) off using a stretchy cast-off method.

Finishing

Sleeve gusset: In the MC and using 4.5mm (US 7) needles, pick up and knit 5 (6, 7, 7) sts from the sleeve hole. Knit 5 rows in stocking stitch. Use kitchener stitch to join the sts together with the sleeve sts on the stitch holder. Sew the sides of the gussets to the body (the gussets give the sweater room for movement). Repeat for the other sleeve. Sew in the ends.

Wet the sweater in lukewarm water, shape it, and leave it to dry flat.

TIP

Before you begin, measure the length of your dog's back and their chest to check whether or not you need to adjust the length and/or width of the sweater.

A genotype is a kind of genetic fingerprint that is the foundation of all human, animal and other life. Our genetic information is stored in the double helix of our DNA. Humans and animals have some similar and some different DNA, but all of our genes are bound to this DNA helix. Our building blocks are encoded within it, a framework for what makes me me and you you. In this pattern, I wanted to visualize what we and our animal friends are made of.

TIIA REHO /
SYSIVILLA
IG sysivilla
RAVELRY Tiia Reho

for humans

Shown in size S
Sizes: XS (S, M, L) (XL, 2XL, 3XL, 4XL)
Recommended ease 8–12cm

vvvvvvvvvvvvvvvvvvvvvvvvvvvvvvvvvvvvvvvvvvvvvvvvv

Measurements of finished sweater
Chest circumference: 80 (90, 100, 109)
(118, 129, 140, 149)cm
Front length from armpit to hem: 33 (35, 35, 40)
(40, 45, 45, 50)cm
Front length, neck to hem: 51 (53, 53, 58)
(58, 63, 63, 68)cm
Upper sleeve circumference: 27 (28.5, 30, 30)
(31, 32, 33, 33)cm
Wrist circumference: 18 (18, 20, 20) (20, 22, 22, 22)cm
Underarm sleeve length: 40 (42, 42, 42)
(42, 44, 44, 44)cm

vvvvvvvvvvvvvvvvvvvvvvvvvvvvvvvvvvvvvvvvvvvvvvvvv

Yarn
*Jalovilla Uuhi (100% wool; 230m/100g) or equivalent DK
weight yarn*
MC: Vanamo 4 (5, 6, 6) (7, 7, 8, 8) hanks or 890
(1100, 1225, 1335) (1445, 1580, 1715, 1825)m
CC1: Kulta (brown) 1 (1, 1, 1) (1, 1, 1, 1) hank or 41 (51, 56, 61)
(66, 73, 79, 84)m
CC2: Poliisi (blue) 1 (1, 1, 1) (1, 1, 1, 1) hank or 41 (51, 56, 61)
(66, 73, 79, 84)m

vvvvvvvvvvvvvvvvvvvvvvvvvvvvvvvvvvvvvvvvvvvvvvvvv

Notions and tension (gauge)
Needles: 80cm and 100cm circular needles in sizes 3mm
(US 2.5) and 3.5mm (US 4)
You will also need: Stitch markers (one openable), stitch
holders or spare yarn, tapestry needle
Tension: 20 sts and 26 rows = 10 x 10cm in stocking
(stockinette) stitch on 3.5mm (US 4) needles, lightly
blocked. Knit a swatch in colourwork and adjust your
needle size if necessary.

for cats

Shown in size 2
Sizes: 1 (2, 3)
Size 1: For cats weighing 2.5–3.5kg
Size 2: For cats weighing 3.5–4.5kg
Size 3: For cats weighing 4.5–5.5kg

Neck circumference: 24 (28, 32)cm
Chest circumference: 38 (42, 44)cm
Waist circumference: 38 (42, 44)cm
Back length: 20.5 (20.5, 22.5)cm

*Jalovilla Uuhi (100% wool; 230m/100g) or equivalent DK
weight yarn*
MC: Vanamo 1 (1, 1) hank or 140 (155, 170)m
CC1: Kulta 1 (1, 1) hank or 12 (13, 14)m
CC2: Poliisi 1 (1, 1) hank or 12 (13, 14)m

Needles: 100cm circular needles in size 3mm (US 2.5) and
3.5mm (US 4) (the entire sweater is knitted using the magic
loop technique)
You will also need: Stitch marker, stitch holders or spare
yarn, tapestry needle
Tension: 20 sts and 26 rows = 10 x 10cm stocking stitch
on 3.5mm (US 4) needles, lightly blocked. Knit a swatch in
colourwork and adjust your needle size if necessary.

Helix is a rather loose and classic boxy sweater that suits a wide range of bodies. The design has deep ribbing at the hem and cuffs, and features a decorative narrow pattern in the yoke. Otherwise, the sweater is worked in plain stocking stitch in one colour, which allows the beautiful helix pattern to shine. This sweater is great for indoor use but can be used as a middle layer outdoors.

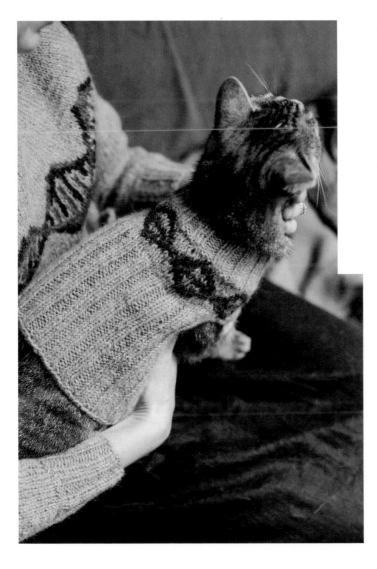

Helix for humans

Body

Using 3mm (US 2.5) 80cm (32in) circular needles and the MC, cast on 80 (88, 100, 108) (116, 128, 140, 148) sts from one hank and then another 80 (88, 100, 108) (116, 128, 140, 148) sts from another hank, so you have two sets of knitting on one set of needles. Attach an openable stitch marker to one of the pieces; this will be the sweater front. Do not join in the round; knit both sections flat separately as follows:

Row 1 (RS): Repeat *k2, p2* until the end of the row.

Row 2 (WS): Repeat *k2, p2* until the end of the row.

Repeat rows 1–2 until the ribbing measures 8cm for the front panel and 10cm for the back panel. End on a WS row.

Swap to 3.5mm (US 4) circular needles.

Join the back and front sections in the round as follows:

Knit the back sts, increase 0 (2, 0, 1) (2, 1, 0, 1) sts, PM (this is the round marker on the left side), knit the front sts, increase 0 (2, 0, 1) (2, 1, 0, 1) sts, knit to the end of the round.

You should now have 160 (180, 200, 218) (236, 258, 280 298) sts. Continue in stocking (stockinette) stitch until the front section measures 33 (35, 35, 40) (40, 45, 45, 50)cm from the bottom of the ribbing.

Next round: Knit until 6 (7, 8, 8) (9, 10, 11, 11) sts remain. Place the next 13 (15, 17, 17) (18, 20, 22, 22) sts onto a stitch holder or spare yarn (removing the marker).

Sleeves

Using 3mm (US 2.5) 100cm (40in) circular needles, cast on 36 (36, 40, 40) (40, 44, 44, 44) sts in the MC. Join in the round for magic loop knitting, PM to mark the start of the round.

Work *k2, p2* ribbing until the work measures 8cm.

Swap to 3.5mm (US 4) needles and work in stocking stitch.

Knit 1 round, evenly increasing 4 (5, 4, 6) (6, 4, 6, 6) sts. You should now have 40 (41, 44, 46) (46, 48, 50, 50 sts. Begin the main shaping.

Increase round: k1, M1L, knit until 1 st remains, M1R, k1.

[2 sts increased]

Repeat the increase round every 11th (10th, 11th, 11th) (11th, 11th, 11th, 11th) round 6 (7, 7, 6) (7, 7, 7, 7)more times. You should now have 54 (57, 60, 60) (62, 64, 66, 66) sts.

Continue in stocking stitch until the sleeve measures 40 (42, 42, 42) (42, 44, 44, 44)cm.

Next round: Knit until 6 (7, 8, 8) (9, 10, 11, 11) sts remain. Put the next 13 (15, 17, 17) (18, 20, 22, 22) sts onto a stitch holder (removing the marker).

Set aside the remaining 41 (42, 43, 43) (44, 44, 44, 44) sleeve sts.

Repeat for the other sleeve.

The sweater is knitted in the round from hem to armpit and the sleeves are knitted separately. The yoke and neck are knitted last once the parts have been joined together on the same set of circular needles. You can knit the entire sweater on circular needles using the magic loop technique.

Yoke

Combine the body and the sleeves:

Using 3.5mm (US 4) long circular needles and the MC, knit the 41 (42, 43, 43) (44, 44, 44, 44) sts for the left sleeve, knit 67 (75, 83, 92) (100, 109, 118, 127) sts for the body (front). Place the next 13 (15, 17, 17) (18, 20, 22, 22) sts onto a stitch holder. Knit the 41 (42, 43, 43) (44, 44, 44, 44) sts for the other sleeve, knit the 67 (75, 83, 92) (100, 109, 118, 127) sts for the body (back). Join in the round, PM at the start of the round (between the back panel and left sleeve). You should now have 216 (234, 252, 270) (288, 306, 324, 342) sts.

Begin to knit the chart:

You can add (I recommend it!) stitch markers every 36 sts (to mark the start of pattern repeats). The pattern repeats 6 (6.5, 7, 7.5) (8, 8.5, 9, 9.5) times per round. **Note:** For sizes S, L, 2XL and 4XL, the final repeat of the pattern is half a repeat, so only knit sts 1–18.

Knit all rows of the chart, unless otherwise indicated in the chart. In the bottom and upper parts of the pattern, trap the floats by working the MC over or under other colours. (Do not trap the floats at the same point in consecutive rows.) After completing the chart, cut the CCs and continue in the MC. You can turn the sweater inside out to knit the yoke so that the floats (on the wrong side of the sweater) are not pulled too tight.

You should now have 72 (78, 84, 90) (80, 85, 90, 95) sts.

Knit 1 round. On the next round, evenly decrease 0 (2, 8, 10) (0, 5, 6, 11) sts. You should now have 72 (76, 76, 80) (80, 80, 84, 84) sts.

Neck

Swap to 3mm (US 2.5) circular needles. Work *k2, p2* ribbing for 12cm.

Cast (bind) off using the Icelandic method:

k1, *place the knitted stitch back on the needle purlwise, put the tip of the right needle through the first stitch on the left needle, stretching it, and then knit the second stitch on the left needle through it, slip both sts from the left needle*. Repeat *–* until 1 st remains, cut the yarn and pull it through the remaining stitch.

Finishing

Close the armpits using the three-needle cast-off and weave the ends in on the WS. Block to your desired measurements and steam or press through gauze. Leave to dry flat.

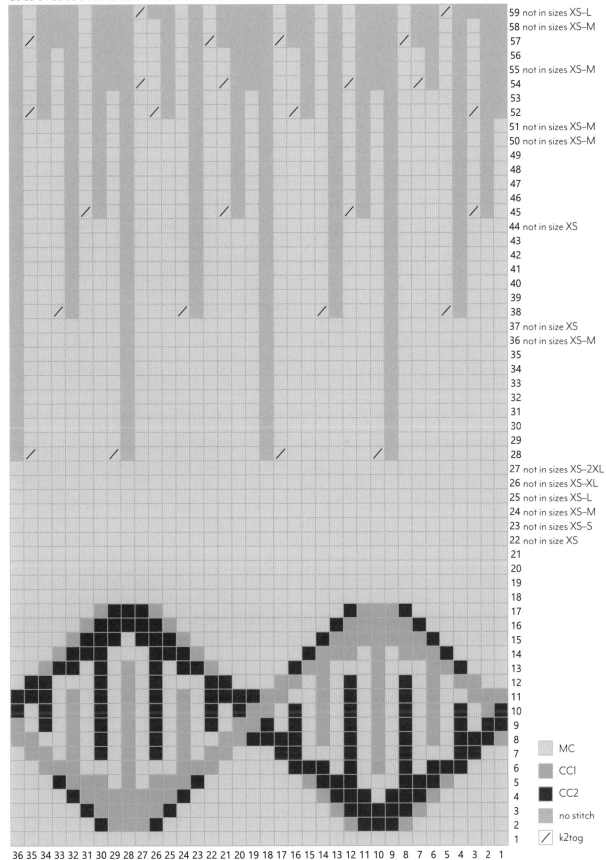

36 35 34 33 32 31 30 29 28 27 26 25 24 23 22 21 20 19 18 17 16 15 14 13 12 11 10 9 8 7 6 5 4 3 2 1

59 not in sizes XS–L
58 not in sizes XS–M
57
56
55 not in sizes XS–M
54
53
52
51 not in sizes XS–M
50 not in sizes XS–M
49
48
47
46
45
44 not in size XS
43
42
41
40
39
38
37 not in size XS
36 not in sizes XS–M
35
34
33
32
31
30
29
28
27 not in sizes XS–2XL
26 not in sizes XS–XL
25 not in sizes XS–L
24 not in sizes XS–M
23 not in sizes XS–S
22 not in size XS
21
20
19
18
17
16
15
14
13
12
11
10
9
8
7
6
5
4
3
2
1

MC
CC1
CC2
no stitch
/ k2tog

Mini Helix for cats

Body

Using 3mm (US 2.5) circular needles, loosely cast on 48 (56, 64) sts in the MC. Join in the round, PM to mark the start of the round (centre front).

Work *k2, p2* ribbing for 5cm (or 10cm if you want a collar that folds over).

Swap to 3.5mm (US 4) circular needles. Knit 1 round, evenly increasing 2 (4, 6) sts. You should now have 50 (60, 70) sts.

Begin to knit the chart:

The pattern repeats 2.5 (3, 3.5) times per round.

Note: For sizes 1 and 3, the final repeat is a half-repeat, so only work sts 1–12 (initially 3–12).

At the top and bottom of the pattern, trap floats every 3–4 sts by working the MC over or under. Make sure that the floats are not too tight (you can make this easier by turning the work inside out so that the floats travel on the outside as you knit – but still on the wrong side). Keep the dominant colour closest to the work.

After the chart, you should have 56 (66, 78) sts. Cut the CCs and continue in stocking stitch in the MC.

Note: If you intend for your cat to wear the sweater for walks on a lead, measure where the lead attaches to the harness (measure between the neck and front legs on the back where the bottom edge of the ribbing is). At this point on the back, cast (bind) off 2 sts and, in the next round, cast on 2 new sts.

Knit 1 round, evenly increasing 12 (12, 10) sts. You should now have 68 (78, 88) sts.

Now knit short rows:

Row 1 (RS): k15 (15, 15), turn.

Row 2 (WS): DS, purl to round marker, SM, p15 (15, 15), turn.

Row 3 (RS): DS, knit to DS, work DS as a single st, turn.

Row 4 (WS): DS, purl to DS, work DS as a single st, turn.

Repeat rows 3–4 one more time.

Next round: DS, knit to round marker, SM.

Make the holes for the sleeves/front-leg holes:

Next round: Knit 5 (6, 7), place 13 (14, 15) sts onto a stitch holder or spare yarn, cast on 13 (14, 15) sts, k32 (38, 44), place 13 (14, 15) sts onto a stitch holder or spare yarn, cast on 13 (14, 15) sts, knit to the end of the round.

Knit 1 round, evenly increasing 8 (6, 0) sts. You should now have 76 (84, 88) sts.

Swap to 3mm (US 2.5) circular needles and work 15 (16, 17)cm of *k2, p2* ribbing. Cast (bind) off loosely.

Sleeve options

Holes for the front legs: Transfer the sleeve sts from the stitch holder or spare yarn onto the needles and loosely cast (bind) off.

Small ribbed sleeves (optional): Transfer the sleeve sts onto 3mm (US 2.5) circular needles and pick up 13 (14, 15) sts from the body sts on the opposite side. Join in the round, PM to mark the start of the round. Knit 1 round in the MC and increase 2 (0, 2) sts. You should now have 28 (28, 32) sts.

Work 4cm of *k2, p2* ribbing and cast off loosely. Repeat for the other sleeve.

Finishing

Weave in the ends on the WS of the work. Block to your desired measurements and steam or press through gauze. Leave to dry.

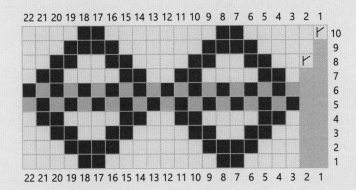

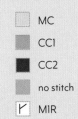

		MC
		CC1
		CC2
		no stitch
		M1R

Mini Helix is a basic jumper for cats. The pattern is a mini version of the Helix sweater for humans, with the double-helix pattern encircling the collar. The rest of the sweater is worked in ribbing, which adapts to the cat's flexibility.

TIP

Leaving holes for the front legs enables your cat to make a wide range of movements, but you can knit small ribbed sleeves, if preferred, following the optional instructions.

TIP

∨∨∨∨∨

The sweater comes in three sizes, for miniature, small and tubbier cats – the ribbing ensures that the fit is flexible. However, you can adjust the sweater further, if needed, and customize it as you see fit.